MAJORING IN SUCCESS

....

Building Your Career While Still in College

FIRST EDITION
ANTHONY J. ARCIERI
MARIANNE E. GREEN

OCTAMERON
ASSOCIATES

Acknowledgments

Heartfelt thanks and gratitude to my friends and family who have been a wonderful inspiration to me, especially my parents, Joseph and Frances Arcieri, my sister Michelle Arcieri, and Kate Gunnoe, without whose support this project would not be possible.

—Anthony J. Arcieri

This project would not have come to fruition without the encouragement, cheers and support of my husband, John Green and my cousin, Phyllis Magaziner. Thanks to you both!

—Marianne E. Green

Book and cover design by Bremmer & Goris Communications, Inc.
Illustrations by Gregory G. Gersch

Address correspondence to:

Octameron Associates
PO Box 2748
Alexandria, VA 22301
703. 836. 5480 (voice)
703. 836. 5650 (fax)

www.octameron.com
info@octameron.com

ISBN 1-57509-046-5
PRINTED IN THE UNITED STATES OF AMERICA

CONTENTS

INTRODUCTION
■■■■■■■■■■■■■■■■■■■■■■■■■■■■■■

"College can be a time-out from the real world
or it can be a head start into the real world"

—Adele Scheele

Majoring in Success: Building Your Career While Still in College is a set of blueprints for designing a rich college experience; one that provides a variety of opportunities for personal growth, skill development, and enhanced employability. It is based on the notion that the college classroom is only one of many learning environments with the potential to both enrich your life while in school, and expand your opportunities after graduation.

Information about a college's regular curriculum and graduation requirements is easy to find. Your counselors, professors and advisors will flood you with material and advice about majors, classroom procedures, exams and degree requirements. You may have to probe a little, however, to find out more about the "second curriculum"—activities, clubs, work-study opportunities, internships, cooperative education, mentor programs, field experience, volunteer work, part-time jobs and summer employment. Yet, it is active participation in this second curriculum that will equip you with the necessary tools to help you discover who you are, what makes you tick, what skills you have and need, what career you'd like to pursue in the future, and what employers might be interested in you.

While still interested in students' classroom success and good grades, employers who recruit on campus report an escalating concern with students' leadership roles, work experience, internships, and community involvement as a measure of their skills and abilities, and as a predictor of future on-the-job success. Gone are the days when a good transcript alone determined employability!

The workplace of the new millennium will require self-directed, skilled, life-long learners who can adapt to change, keep pace with rapid innovations in technology, and have the "know how" to take charge of their working lives. These essential traits and abilities—building blocks of success—can be practiced and polished from the first day of your freshmen year to the last day of your senior year through active involvement in activities and projects outside the college classroom, as well as inside.

You may not be able to control what the future will bring, but you can control what you will bring to the future!

What are the benchmarks of a successful college career? There are at least two. On graduation day you will be awarded your "sheepskin," that piece of paper you worked so hard to earn, announcing to the world that you have fulfilled all of the academic requirements for a bachelor's degree. Just as important, though, will be your record of leadership, community service, related work experience, activities, and skills. The symbol of these accomplishments will come in the form of a dynamic resume, one which will capture the attention of potential employers.

The remainder of this book will help provide you with the tools to build your second curriculum, and guide you along the path to college success.

CHAPTER 1

■ ■ ■ ■ ■ ■ ■ ■ ■ ■ ■ ■ ■ ■ ■ ■ ■ ■ ■

GETTING TO KNOW THE COLLEGE
CAREER OFFICE:
PROGRAMS AND SERVICES

Give a man a fish and he'll eat for a day,
But teach a man to fish and he'll eat for a lifetime.

—Anonymous

As a high school senior trying to pinpoint the right college to attend, post-college career plans and job placement probably seem far off in the misty future. You've heard or read that colleges have career offices to help seniors find jobs, but right now you are a long way from that stage. Besides, there's so much to focus on that affects you right now—college application deadlines, choice of major, financial aid forms, housing decisions and other compelling topics.

You realize that a fundamental reason for attending college is to equip yourself for employment in the new millennium, but to paraphrase Scarlett O'Hara in *Gone with the Wind*, you'll worry about careers tomorrow!

Case Study ═══════════════════════════════

The Cortez family threads its way among the information tables at the State University Preview Fair. They are spending the day on campus trying to find out as much as possible about State to decide whether John, a high school junior, should apply for admission in the future. They have collected information and talked with college officials about admissions, housing, financial aid, student activities and health services. The one table they avoid is the Career Services information table, stacked with brochures and hand-outs. "First I have to pick a major and then I'll think about my career; I'm not even a freshman yet," John tells his parents as they pass by.

John is shortsighted in postponing contact with State University's career office; in fact, his criteria for college selection should include an evaluation of the services and resources provided by this very important office. Like most high school students (as well as some college students), John lacks a full understanding of how career offices typically operate or the array of services they offer, services designed to help all students—freshmen, sophomores, juniors and seniors—lay the groundwork for future career success.

Finding Out About College Career Services

Prospective college students can start their fact-finding mission by locating basic information about career offices (referred to on some campuses as Career Planning and Placement, the Career Development Office, and the Career Services Center) in college catalogues and view books, usually in the section dealing with student affairs. In addition to carefully reading this descriptive material, pick up relevant handouts from career office tables at college fairs and stop to ask a few questions such as:

- What career services do you have for college freshmen?
- How can you help me choose a major or decide on a career?

- How do I go about getting an internship?
- What are career options for someone with a _____ major?

The response you receive from career advisors who staff the table should be friendly and informative. Ask for business cards so you can call or e-mail with questions that occur to you after the event is over. If your campus visit includes a tour, ask to see where the career office is located. If you call ahead, you can sometimes arrange individual appointments with career advisors to coincide with your visit.

A quick and easy way to learn more about career services is to check out the career office's Web site for each college that interests you. These beneficial Web pages list staff data, events, procedures, programs, internship sites, job information, and links to other useful Internet sites.

For example, the University of Delaware's Career Services Center's Web site has more than two hundred pages of helpful, up-to-date and varied career-related material reachable from any computer with Internet access. This information is organized into the following general categories:

- Who We Are
- What's Happening
- Services for Students & Alumni
- Services for Employers
- Graduate School Information
- Internet Resources

Browsing this and other college career office URLs provide a wealth of information about career services and careers.

Your research will quickly show that career offices today are very different in philosophy and function from the "placement" offices your parents may remember from their college experience. Once upon a time career offices emphasized "placing" graduating seniors—primarily business and engineering majors—in full-time jobs through on-campus interview programs and job fairs. Now college career offices provide progressive and comprehensive services and resources to help students of all majors— freshmen, sophomores, juniors and seniors—develop the skills they need to seek satisfying employment throughout their life span. There are still rewarding opportunities for seniors to interact and interview with employers, but the focus has broadened to include the career planning needs of a diverse student body. To use an analogy, career offices today are committed to teaching students *how* to fish, rather than catching a fish for them!

In some large universities, the career office is decentralized; that is, different schools or departments within the university maintain their own career centers. At the University of Texas, for example, the business school operates a self-contained office for its majors. On other campuses, the career office is centralized, serving all majors. In this set up, career advisors are usually assigned to work with specific academic departments—coordinating job fairs, leading workshops, making in-class presentations and advising students. Your investigation will also show that in some universities, career testing, and preliminary career counseling are handled by the college counseling center. On other campuses, the career office deals with all career-related matters. Understanding how a college career office operates *before* you come to campus will make it easier to get involved early on and take full advantage of all career services!

An Overview of Career Services

Right from the start of your college career you can begin to utilize many of the programs and services offered by your career office. Even though staff size, facilities, organization, technology and operating budgets vary from campus to campus, some form of comparable service will be available to you, though it may be called a different name. Be persistent, read the literature, check-out the Web site and ask lots of questions; before long you'll be in-the-know about career services on your college campus. Here's a sampling of what you'll find:

Career Testing

Students who are undecided about a major or career often find it helpful to take interest or personality inventories using a paper-and-pencil or computerized format. While these tests don't provide definitive answers, they can be helpful in developing self-insight in addition to opening your eyes to majors and careers you haven't yet considered, or confirming your hunches about the best future career for you.

Career Advice

Career counselors and advisors can provide reassurance, encouragement, new perspectives and valuable information to assist you with all aspects of the career planning and employment process. Call or stop by the career office to schedule an appointment; some offices have "drop-in" appointments, while others require a pre-set meeting time.

Resources

The library at your career office will be stocked with books, brochures, videos, computer resources, surveys, and handouts on many of the more than 20,000 possible jobs. Do you want to know what careers are open to English majors? Are you curious about the salary of a television news reporter? Do you want to find internships listings in the field of advertising in New York City? Your college career library will provide up-to-date information.

Shadowing/Mentor Program

Many colleges can arrange for you to "shadow" alumni working in occupations of interest to you. Ask them how they got started in their profession, what they like best or least about their position, and what a typical day is like. Students who are unsure about their career paths often find these visits enlightening.

Part-time Employment

You may need to work part-time during the school year to help pay your college expenses. Many career offices search out part-time jobs for students and post the openings on bulletin boards, in notebooks, and on-line.

Volunteer Fairs and Experiences

Career offices also post on-campus and community volunteer opportunities in notebooks and on bulletin boards, or sponsor volunteer fairs where community agencies are invited to interact with and recruit college students for volunteer positions.

Resume Preparation Workshops and Critiques

You will probably need a resume for summer employment, internships, scholarship applications, etc., so check the career office newsletter or Web site to find out about resume (and cover letter) writing workshops. Once you have completed a rough draft of your resume, make an appointment to have it critiqued by a career advisor. The comments and suggestions of a professional will ensure that your resume is the best it can be.

Summer Jobs

Your search for summer employment will be aided by the job listings posted at the career office or linked to its Web site. Summer job search workshops will also help you locate positions that will be enriching both financially and personally!

Internships/Field Experience/Co-op

Many career offices sponsor internship fairs to introduce students to local internship opportunities with nonprofits, for profits, or government agencies. Career libraries usually contain directories of internships and co-op jobs in every field, nationally and internationally. Nowadays, information on internships is also linked to the career office's Web site. Talk to a career advisor about obtaining credit for your internship.

Graduate School Information

Are you interested in learning more about graduate programs in law, medicine, business, psychology, English, or some other field? Attend career office-sponsored graduate school fairs which host admission staffs from professional and graduate schools around the country. Career libraries and Internet sites also contain resources to help you prepare for your post-graduate options. It's never too early to explore your future!

Workshops on Job Search and Interviewing Techniques

Sign up for workshops on conducting a thorough job search and practicing your interviewing strategies. These skills will prove invaluable in landing part-time jobs, internships, and summer jobs as well as full-time post-graduate positions.

Career Week Programs

October and April are prime months for Career Weeks! The career office generally puts together a week of special career-related programming for students of every major during these months. Even with a busy schedule, try to make room to attend a few events. Listen to alumni speak about their jobs in panel discussions. Take part in a fashion show that showcases the latest professional attire. Get some interview tips during a workshop. Meet the employers at the job fair.

Full-Time Job Listings

Full-time jobs may be listed in binders or file folders, posted on the Web site, published in newsletters or maintained on a telephone hotline. Find out how your career office posts full-time jobs and familiarize yourself with current job openings in your field, even though you aren't ready to apply for a full-time job yet.

Resume Referral Service

On most campuses, career offices respond to employers looking for summer or full-time help by sending them resumes of students who are registered with the office. Some career offices receive thousands of requests for student resumes each year. Find out how to qualify for this important service. Even freshman can make good use of the resume-mailing service when they are looking for summer positions, particularly in the fields of computer science, business and engineering.

On-Campus Interview Program

Each year, thousands of recruiters from business and industry travel to college career offices around the country to hold information sessions and interview graduating seniors for full-time career positions. Employers as diverse as IBM, Lord & Taylor, the FBI (and CIA), Anderson Consulting, J.P. Morgan, the Peace Corps and K-Mart conduct thirty-minute screening interviews with qualified candidates whom they have usually pre-selected. Candidates who excel in this process are invited to interview further at the company site. Some recruiters search for specific majors to fill their company's job openings while others are open to students of every possible major. Students who take advantage of on-campus interviewing usually find it a very rewarding experience.

Job Fairs

Job fairs are a popular way for employers and students to exchange information and network. Organizational representatives are invited to campus to staff booths or tables and converse informally with students who circulate around the room. Occasionally, brief interviews take place, as well. Some universities may sponsor ten or more job fairs annually that cater to the needs of different student populations, for example: Project Search for Teachers, Health and Nursing Career Fair; the Agriculture Career Day; All Majors Job Fair; Fashion Opportunities Day; Nonprofit and

Human Services Fair, etc. Students at all levels are usually welcomed at these important events.

Reference Mailing Service

Some career offices maintain students' letters of reference and student teaching reports in a file for a designated period of time, and send out copies of these documents to employers or graduate schools at the students' request. Education and health-related majors are the predominant users of reference mailing services.

Start Early

Career decision-making and preparation, like studying for an exam, should not be left until the last minute. It's up to you to set the process in motion: explore your college's career office, meet and stay in touch with career advisors, and take full advantage of career programs and events from your freshman year forward. Why? Your future depends on it!

CHAPTER 2

∎∎∎∎∎∎∎∎∎∎∎∎∎∎∎∎∎∎∎

MYTHS ABOUT COLLEGE AND CAREERS

"We judge ourselves by our capabilities.
Others judge us by what we have done."

—Henry Wadsworth Longfellow

You and you parents probably share some misconceptions about the relationship between college and careers; misconceptions which can lead to disappointment and confusion as your senior year unfolds and post-graduation plans are in the air.

While college courses and curricula certainly contribute to your fund of knowledge and basic credentials, it is often the experiences and skills you acquire outside the classroom that attract the interest and attention of employers. Too many bright students lose out on good jobs because their resumes reflect little real-world experience.

Case Study

Andrew, a senior English major, worked hard throughout his college years. An honors student, he completed a thesis on a 16th century poet. In his junior year, he was invited by his professors to present at a national conference and served as a teaching assistant for a freshman composition class. Andrew never received less than an A- on any of his papers. He devoted so much time to his studies, however, that participation in any activities or community service was out of the question. During the summers, he waited tables at a local restaurant to earn spending money, and took courses at a nearby college.

By the second semester of his senior year, Andrew was eager to tackle the job search process. While he knew that graduate school in English literature was a future possibility, he was tired of school and wanted some real world work experience first. Since he had confidence in his writing ability, he looked at jobs in advertising, news reporting, or editing, sending his resume out in response to newspaper advertisements and on-line job listings. He also attended job fairs and interviewed for technical writing positions through the on-campus interview program.

The results were disappointing. Andrew received few invitations to interview for the positions he found in newspapers and on-line. His conversations at the career fair and his on-campus interviews led nowhere. Andrew found that employers were visibly impressed by his sterling academic record, but were put-off by his lack of career-related skills. Most employers wanted to see writing samples illustrating the application of his writing skills to real world situations. Copies of Andrew's term papers just wouldn't do.

Both Andrew and his parents were confused and concerned. Andrew had excelled in his classes, achieved honors, and been lauded by his professors, yet he had difficulty demonstrating to

*employers how his skills would transfer into the workplace and
help them solve their real world problems. He was passed over in
favor of students whose resumes showed related internships,
jobs, volunteer work and leadership but who did not have his
high record of academic achievement. What had gone wrong?*

College is still about academic achievement—and hard work in that arena
will certainly be rewarded. But academic work alone is no longer sufficient.
Andrew might have made more effective choices during his college career if
he and his parents had been aware of some of the common myths about the
connection between college and career.

Myth #1
A college degree guarantees a good job.

Few parents, and even fewer students, still see the college degree as an
automatic ticket to a good job. The steadily increasing pool of college
graduates has served to inflate the entry level requirements for sales,
service, managerial, and other positions from a high school diploma, a
generation ago, to a bachelor's degree in the 1990s. Even though college
graduates tend to earn higher salaries in the course of their working lives,
and have more opportunities for advancement and job mobility than high
school graduates, the bachelor's degree by itself cannot and does not
guarantee satisfying and well-paid employment.

Myth #2
Good grades in college ensure a good job.

Employers still use your grade point average as an indicator of your
ability to assimilate information, your aptitude for learning, and your
propensity for hard work. By achieving recognition through academic
scholarships, Dean's List, and election to honorary societies, you boost
employers' confidence in your ability to grasp and absorb new information
and apply it on the job. But employers also consider other skills and
abilities in selecting new hires. The National Association of Colleges and
Employers cites several employer surveys which rank interpersonal skills,
teamwork, communications skills, leadership skills, and related work
experience as very important criteria in evaluating college students for full-
time positions (*Job Choices* 1999). These skills are usually developed

through the second college curriculum, experiences beyond the classroom, laboratory or lecture hall.

Myth #3

Your college major determines your future job.

All majors are created equal in that they provide a rigorous, in-depth look at an area of scholarship. Some majors, however, come equipped with built-in second-curriculum opportunities because they are linked to specific careers. For example, a nursing curriculum includes both a theoretical classroom component and hands-on experiences in a hospital setting. The same is true for education majors; classroom work is complemented by student teaching experience in an actual elementary or high school classroom. Nursing and education are examples of majors which blaze a clear path toward a specific career. Business and engineering majors also tend to be more job-oriented.

Conversely, liberal arts majors, especially in the humanities (English, history, foreign language, art history, music, etc.) and social sciences (sociology, psychology, anthropology, political science, international relations, geography, etc.) are usually structured to match up with areas of academic scholarship, rather than careers. Even math and science majors do not usually include real world applications as part of the curricula—the emphasis is generally on information acquisition and research methodology.

Does that mean only students in "job-linked" majors are employable? Of course not. Other students just have to be more conscious about supplementing their majors with hands-on, practical experiences. In fact, no matter what you decide to major in, it is still up to you, the student, to shoulder the responsibility of investigating career options and developing career-related skills by being proactive: joining the student chapter of Save the Whales, working on a senatorial campaign, pursuing a summer job at Du Pont Pharmaceuticals, volunteering at the animal shelter, interning at the Department of Corrections or shadowing an alumnus during his day on the job as a corporate lawyer. You just can't depend on your academic major and college curriculum to build the necessary bridges to career options and future employment!

In today's booming job market, recruiters for sales, marketing, managerial, public relations, human resources, technical writing and social services positions are willing and eager to interview graduating seniors with any major, as long as candidates appear to have the required aptitude, skills and experience to succeed in training and on the job.

Myth #4

Campus and community activities are frills; only paid work experience counts for your future.

Far from it! Employers and graduate school admission staffs don't see out-of-class activities as a diversion from the central mission of college; rather, they are quick to acknowledge that the second curriculum offers a powerful source of learning, skill development and experience. A recent survey of 548 recruiters at Florida State University found that eighty-six percent of the respondents rated leadership in student organizations as very important or above average in their candidate-selection decisions. An even higher number of recruiters—eighty-eight percent—judged students' job-related experience to be very important. Clearly, students' out-of-class involvement with leadership roles and related work exposure, whether volunteer or paid, is critically important to employers when choosing entry level hires from the pool of college graduates.

A study of graduating seniors at San Francisco State University indicated that more than half of all students who received job offers attributed their success to the internships and volunteer experience they had pursued during their undergraduate years.

It is the quality of experience, paid or volunteer, that determines personal growth, skill development and commitment to the profession. In high demand fields such as engineering or computer science, interns are often paid for their efforts. In other fields, volunteer work and unpaid jobs must pave the way to enhanced experience and future job possibilities. But you can count on the fact that employers recognize the value of all relevant experience!

Balancing your academic work load with extracurricular activities can be challenging. At first, it might be difficult to fit classes, study hours and activities into one short day. Pick one or two activities your freshman year, and use school breaks and summer vacations productively—you will reap the rewards. In fact, there is evidence that, while creating some additional pressures and competing priorities, extracurricular activities like internships and co-ops force you to better manage your time, which enhances academic performance and increases your likelihood of graduation.

Myth #5

Someone in charge at your college or university will make sure you take the necessary steps to plan your career.

From the first day of freshman orientation, through the last day of senior year finals, the only person at your school in charge of activating your future is you! This is true even if you have no idea what you want to do after graduation. Student services such as career and counseling services, student activities offices, faculty advisors, volunteer centers, foreign study offices, etc. can help you along the way, but the onus is on you to set the process in motion and monitor your progress. If you want magic, you have to be the magician. College will provide you with sources of knowledge, contacts, creativity, and opportunity, but you have to take advantage of them. A passive, wait-and-see attitude will blind you to the rich array of possibilities that college can offer.

College isn't a rehearsal for real life. It is real life.

CHAPTER 3

■■■■■■■■■■■■■■■■■■

CAREER ASSESSMENT

"There is no future in any job.
The future lies in the one who holds the job."

—George Crane

Before you set out to find that perfect internship or spend some time volunteering, take a moment to learn a little bit about yourself. This chapter covers Career Assessment—the method by which you discover your interests and abilities, and translate them into possible careers. We hope this will spark some thoughts in you, and prepare you for the next few chapters dealing with options that will help you "Major in Success!"

Four-Step Model

Generally speaking, career development models follow four steps.

Step One

Analyze your interests, skills, abilities, values, and goals while gathering information on the world of work.

The resulting combination of self-knowledge and work information will help you focus your activity search, and lead you toward a potential career. Even if you remain undecided after the assessment exercises, you should still come away with a better understanding of yourself and of what your background can predict for your future.

Step Two

Explore different careers.

During this phase, spend some time reading literature on fields that interest you. You may choose to browse the career information in your campus career center or counseling center. It is also a good opportunity to look at the different majors available to you on campus, and learn how each major translates to a comparable career. Programs like "Day on the Job" or other shadowing experiences can give you an insider's view of a workplace environment.

Step Three

Experience different career possibilities.

This phase, the subject of most of this book, is crucial in helping you add and remove career possibilities from your "master list." Internships, part-time jobs, volunteer experiences, and campus activities give you a "kick the tires" practical method of determining which career is right for you and provide you with marketable experience when graduation rolls around.

Step Four

Use your college career center to search for post-graduation jobs.

Whether you decide to attend graduate school or work full-time, the implementation phase is your opportunity to put all your knowledge to the test. You will be utilizing the campus interviewing program, following up on job leads, and attending job fairs.

Worksheet One: Assess the Situation...

To better understand yourself, in the context of career possibilities, think to the past and the present, as well as to the future. What are your *achievements* (past successes)? What are your *abilities*? (present ability to perform a task)? What are your *aptitudes* (probable future level of ability to perform a task)?

Adding these together, determine your *interests*. This will direct you to appropriate internships and activities, and eventually to your future career. Complete the exercise below to help you organize your thoughts about where you stand in your career assessment.

Achievements

What recognitions have you received in the following categories?

Academic Honors or Awards

_____

_____

_____

_____

_____

Sports/Teamwork Commendations

_____

_____

_____

_____

Special Recognition at your part-time job

_____

_____

_____

_____

Volunteer Work that meant something to you

_____

_____

_____

_____

_____

Abilities

Do you have these skills? Think of places you exhibited them, and how you did so:

Clerical Skills

_____

_____

_____

_____

_____

_____

Computer / Technical Skills

_____

_____

_____

_____

_____

_____

Public Speaking / Writing / Communication Skills

_____

_____

_____

_____

_____

_____

Foreign Languages Spoken

_____

_____

_____

_____

_____

_____

Artistic Abilities

_____

_____

_____

_____

_____

_____

Organizational / Management Skills

_____

_____

_____

_____

_____

_____

Aptitudes

Prepare yourself to use these skills; think of places you have practiced them:

Positive Attitude (enthusiasm, eagerness to learn, etc.)

_____

_____

_____

_____

_____

Good Work Ethic (attention to detail, punctuality, etc.)

_____

_____

_____

_____

_____

Verbal / Mathematical Competence

_____

_____

_____

_____

_____

Using the above information on Achievements, Abilities, and Aptitudes, you can now determine where your interests lie.

Worksheet Two: Determine Your Interests

On this worksheet, determine your level of interest for each of the six areas. Then, jot down some examples of how those interests relate to you.

1. Working with your hands
(lawn work, car repair, athletics, etc.)

_____ Very Interested   _____ Somewhat Interested

_____ Interested   _____ Not Interested

My Examples:

_____

_____

2. Lab work, or using numbers
(using a microscope, solving algebraic equations, studying scientific theories, etc.)

_____ Very Interested   _____ Somewhat Interested

_____ Interested   _____ Not Interested

My Examples:

_____

_____

3. Art, writing, music, photography
(sketching, playing an instrument in the band, reading/writing poetry, designing clothes, etc.)

_____ Very Interested   _____ Somewhat Interested

_____ Interested   _____ Not Interested

My Examples:

_____

_____

4. Working with others socially

(teaching, helping, listening to others' troubles, leading group discussions, etc.)

_____ Very Interested   _____ Somewhat Interested

_____ Interested   _____ Not Interested

My Examples:

_____

_____

5. Selling, taking charge, or leading a group

(speaking publicly, organizing others, getting people to do things your way, influencing, etc.)

_____ Very Interested   _____ Somewhat Interested

_____ Interested   _____ Not Interested

My Examples:

_____

_____

6. Working on computers or in an office environment

(perform bookkeeping, filling out tax forms, keeping accurate records, operating business machines, etc.)

_____ Very Interested   _____ Somewhat Interested

_____ Interested   _____ Not Interested

My Examples:

_____

_____

What Does It All Mean?

Now that you have indicated which interest areas appeal to you, read the descriptions below of your top three interests. See if these descriptions sound familiar to you...this will help you focus on majors, internships, and eventually on your first job!

Working with your hands

People in this category may prefer outdoor activities or those that center around the systematic handling of tools, animals, or machines. They prefer jobs that require motor coordination and skill, but avoid tasks requiring interpersonal and verbal skills. They typically perceive themselves as having athletic, physical, and mechanical ability, but lack ability in expressing emotions, communicating feelings, and human relations.

Occupational Examples: Airplane Mechanic, Firefighter, Fish and Wildlife Specialist, Inspector.

Scientific or mathematical work

Individuals in this interest area typically prefer to work with things and tasks over people. They enjoy solving abstract problems, and prefer to think through problems rather than act them out. These folks generally perceive themselves as scholarly, intellectual, and self-confident, but lacking in leadership ability.

Occupational Examples: Biologist, Meteorologist, Researcher, Astronomer, Editor of a Scientific Journal.

Artistic and creative work

Self-expression is the key to this interest area. Typical activities allow for the manipulation of physical, verbal, or human materials to create art forms. People here prefer to work alone, having a great need for individualistic self-expression. They are typically sensitive and emotional, and are quite original and unique. These folks have little interest in problems that are highly structured or require physical strength. Artistic people may describe themselves as expressive, intuitive, independent, nonconforming, and somewhat disorderly. They value aesthetics. Most in this area have competencies in language, art, drama, music, and writing.

Occupational Examples: Novelist, Actor, Free-Lance Writer, Cartoonist, Composer, Sculptor.

Working in a social environment

This type of person is sociable, responsible, caring, and concerned for the welfare of others. They are adept at self-expression, and value strong interpersonal relationships. They seek to be the center of attention, and prefer to solve problems through discussions with others, or arranging relationships between others. These folks have little interest in manual, scientific, or physical labor. A social person would describe him/herself as cheerful, popular, achieving, and a good leader.

Occupational Examples: High School Teacher, Speech Therapist, Counselor, School Principal, Social Worker.

Selling, leading, taking charge

Someone in this interest area is very energetic; great with words and thus effective in selling, dominating, and leading. These people perceive themselves as adventurous, enthusiastic, self-confident, persuasive, and dominant. They may value money, power, and status and consider political and economic achievement to be important.

Occupational Examples: Buyer, Ad Executive, Life Insurance Salesperson, Store Manager, Business Executive.

Office/Computer Work

This type of individual enjoys ordered and systematic activities (both numerical and verbal). They typically do not seek leadership, but respond well to power and a chain of command. They dislike ambiguity, preferring to know precisely what is expected. They are stable and dependable while being less interested in physical skills or human relationships. They value business, economic achievement, material possessions and status.

Occupational Examples: Accountant, Banker, Tax Expert, Financial Analyst, Credit Investigator, Bookkeeper.

What Now?

Now you have the tools necessary to pursue activities, internships, and part-time jobs while in college. You may even be more aware of what career path you wish to pursue. Take a look at the achievements, abilities, and aptitudes you listed above. What do they say about you? Compare them to your interests. Do you see any patterns? Are you someone who likes a social environment, working with others and helping them in many different ways? Or, are you more introverted, preferring to work alone or with maybe one other person to solve a problem? Maybe you enjoy expressing yourself through artwork or theater. Or perhaps you really enjoy working on the computer or with numbers. All of this information is very helpful, and will provide a glimpse into what direction you will head in these next few years!

Keep in mind, just because you have an interest in something doesn't mean you must pursue a career in that area. For example, you may enjoy working with your hands by helping your older brother fix his car. Does that mean you should be a mechanic? No! If you want to be a mechanic, that's perfectly fine. But your interest actually reveals that you are an independent thinker who likes to solve riddles and manipulate objects to solve a problem. Those words can describe a mechanical engineer, an emergency medical technician, or an electrician. It's important for you to think about your interests, and translate them to work activities.

Now, you should take the time to explore Web sites or career literature in your campus career office or counseling center. Learn about different career paths and how your interests relate to them. You may want to take an assessment test, such as the Strong Interest Inventory. You can probably take it at the Counseling or Career Center. The test will assess your interests, and compare them with the interests of individuals currently in many different professions. That may give you some insight into what other people with like interests are doing with their lives.

But even if you don't take this inventory, spend time checking out the Web sites below. You will gain great insight into yourself, and into the possible career paths awaiting you.

Site Seeing

Catapult Career Assessment Tools
http://www.jobweb.org/catapult/Assess.htm

Provides seven links to sites ranging from personality inventories, to interest assessment, to career planning advice.

Career Key
http://www4.ncsu.edu/unity/lockers/users/l/lkj/

Free on-line version of the Strong Interest Inventory, allowing users to identify career interests and relate them to similar occupations.

VARK

http://www.active-learning-site.com

Great tool to get to know yourself better. Helps you understand how you work with the information you receive from your surroundings by highlighting your preferred learning style for the intake and output of ideas.

Career Interests Game

http://www.missouri.edu/~cppcwww/holland.shtml

Game which helps users discover interests and matches them to possible occupations.

US News and World Report: Find Your Career

http://www.usnews.com/usnews/edu/beyond/bccguide.htm

Descriptions of different occupations, as well as insider advice about what careers are hot and in demand now and down the road.

The Student Center

http://www.aboutwork.com

Broad and detailed site providing job listings, as well as helpful career information. Also includes several on-line tests. Geared toward the college student.

Career Services Center, University of Waterloo

http://www.adm.uwaterloo.ca/infocecs/crc/manual-home.html

Provides plenty of self assessment information, and printable forms for you to fill out as you go.

Keirsey Temperament Scale

http://www.keirsey.com/

On-line personality test, designed to help users learn more about themselves and others. Based on the Myers-Briggs Type Indicator, the test result is a four-letter code revealing your personality type.

Occupational Outlook Handbook

http://stats.bls.gov:80/ocohome.htm

Information source for 200+ of the most popular occupations. Also includes employment projections and information about training and pay.

Careers Online Virtual Careers Show

http://www.careersonline.com.au/show/menu.html

Directory of over 1,000 occupational descriptions divided into 12 categories.

Major Resource Kits

http://www.udel.edu/CSC/mrk.html

Information on over 80 majors and the careers they translate to. Includes information on entry-level job titles, descriptions, major employers in that field, and contacts of associations and professional organizations in those fields.

CHAPTER 4

■■■■■■■■■■■■■■■■■■■■

STUDENT EMPLOYMENT

*"All genuine knowledge originates
from direct experience."*

—Mao Tse-tung

So you're thrilled about getting into your first-choice college or university. You open your admit letter, and jump up and down with excitement as you think ahead to the next four years of college life. Then mom and dad ask, "How are we going to pay for this?" All at once, it hits you—it costs *money* to go to college. In some cases, *a lot* of money.

The good news? If you've applied for financial aid, you will probably be awarded work-study money. And even if you don't qualify for financial aid, you can still earn a few thousand dollars during the school year to help defray college costs. In either case, it will be a good opportunity!

This chapter will introduce you to the pros and cons of student employment. From personal development, to making money, to getting ready for your career, we'll help you with the ins and outs of working on- (and off-) campus—bringing home the bacon, while working on your parchment.

Case Study ══════════════════════════════

*Julia is a sophomore sociology major at a large southern
university. She chose not to work during her freshman year, and
now wishes she had so she could have a few extra dollars to
spend on entertainment and expenses. She was awarded work-
study through the financial aid office, and decided to find a
position on campus for a few hours per week. She found a job in
the advisement center, helping students choose courses, register*

for classes, decide between majors, and become acclimated to the university community. Julia loved this new position. She made some much needed extra money, while helping her fellow students and getting experience at the same time. She was also able to work on her communication skills, and her ability to relate to superiors and co-workers.

This case study is an example of how a work-study award can benefit you as a college student. Approximately 3,300 institutions of higher education provide work-study awards as part of their students' financial aid packages.

What Is Work-Study?

Work-study is a federal program designed to give students the opportunity to work on- or off-campus to help defray college expenses. The college or university, as your employer, benefits from this program because they pay only about 25% of your wages, with the federal government paying the rest.

With this inexpensive and readily available workforce, colleges and universities use student employees in many functional areas on campus. You'll find work-study students serving food in the cafeteria, shelving books in the library, giving out locker keys in the athletic center, and washing test tubes in the laboratories.

Many schools also employ students in financial aid, admissions, career services, counseling, computing, and residence life. Even area non-profit organizations can hire work-study students. Most visible as of late, the "America Reads" program, sponsored by the federal government to encourage students to become reading tutors. Although a worthwhile program, this chapter will focus on on-campus student employment.

Why Work?

Why do students choose to work while in college? There are many reasons; some more obvious than others. A recent study by Yuko Mulugetta and Dennis Chavez cited six motivating factors: First came "money" and "personal fulfillment," followed by "gaining job experience" and "referral contacts," and finally, "social interaction" and "a break from schoolwork."

Studies have also shown that students who work part-time while attending school full-time actually perform better academically than those who do not. Furthermore, they are less likely to drop out. This type of campus involvement contributes to student happiness, necessitates better time management and expands a student's support system. Although some students may want to postpone working until their sophomore year to give themselves time to adjust to college life and academic pressure (that's OK!), the benefit to working during even two of your four college years far outweighs the reasons you may think of not to work.

As you're looking for on-campus work-study positions, think about what you want to gain from the experience. Although some positions involve only menial or mundane tasks, others may be quite beneficial to you personally and professionally. For example, data input might not seem too glamorous, but if the data you're inputting happens to be in the financial aid or student accounts offices, you can pick up information that may help you fill out your forms next year. And, knowing staff members in these important offices will be a huge benefit if you have questions about your aid package or problems arise and you need to cut through the bureaucracy.

This "inside view" of the school is a tangible benefit to working on campus. Students gain a unique perspective of how the college or university really operates, as well as a sense of ownership for their work and for the school. They create a niche for themselves. They increase their social contacts, as they begin establishing relationships with each other and with superiors. And, they learn to balance work and school priorities, and manage time effectively and efficiently. These skills will be invaluable on your first job.

Wages

Depending on your school's location, your pay can run anywhere from minimum wage to $8 per hour. This much needed cash can help you pay tuition, or at least cover expenses like books and travel. But beware: Work-study is not a scholarship! One common pitfall is to assume a $5,000 work-study award means $5,000 will immediately be credited to your account as an award. NO! What it means is that you have been offered the option of working at an on- or off-campus location. The job is subsidized by the federal government, up to that dollar amount for the year. You will be paid via paycheck just like at any other job. What you choose to do with that money (again, like any other job) is up to you. The $5,000 listed on your award letter as "work-study" must be paid to the university up front.

Example:

City University—Office of Financial Aid:

Michelle Williams' Cost of Attendance:	$18,000
Less Expected Family Contribution:	$ 4,500
Remaining Need:	**$13,500**

Breakdown of Award Package:

Alumni Scholarship:	$ 2,500
University Grant:	$ 2,000
Direct Student Loan:	$ 5,000
Federal Work Study:	$ 4,000
Total:	**$13,500**

Amount Due from Family Prior to Enrollment:

Cost of Attendance:	$18,000	
Less Grant and Loans:	$ 9,500	
Balance Due:	**$ 8,500**	($4,500 EFC + $4,000 Work-study)

In this example, Michelle's annual cost of attendance is $18,000 and her financial aid award totals $13,500. At first glance, it seems as though Michelle needs only $4,500 to pay her bills for the school year. Upon closer inspection, however, we see she's been awarded Federal Work-Study. That $4,000 must be paid with the other $4,500 at the time of billing. Then, during the year, Michelle will earn back the $4,000 to use however she wishes, but theoretically to apply toward college expenses. When Michelle has earned that full $4,000, the school will terminate her employment until the following year, unless it is willing to continue paying her without Uncle Sam's 75% subsidy.

Most campus offices will either limit your hours per week, so your award stretches over the entire year, or pick-up the slack when you exceed your work-study dollars.

Tip: Sit down with your parents to find a way to pay the work-study portion of your bill upfront. If your work-study "gift" will be an impossible hardship, ask your school about installment plans. Most institutions will make arrangements for you to spread your payments out over the course of the academic year.

Other Job Options

If you haven't been offered a work-study award as part of your financial aid package, fear not! Many campus offices hire non work-study students. Think about becoming a Resident Assistant, for example. It's a great way to pay your expenses while gaining valuable experience! Most colleges will cover your entire room and board costs, as well as provide you with a monetary stipend. In exchange, you'll counsel students, deal with sensitive or difficult situations, and sharpen your management skills. Regardless of what career field you eventually choose, your experience as an R.A. will enrich your pocketbook, and your resume.

Another good place to work is in the campus career center! What a great way to make a few extra bucks while learning the ropes for your own future job search. Career offices use students to help staff the library, perform resume critiques, conduct resume-writing workshops and provide outreach to the university community. Students work about ten hours per week, and are paid a generous stipend. In exchange, they obtain knowledge that will directly help them in their own job search. By their senior year, their job search, resume-writing and job interviewing skills far surpass those of their classmates giving them a huge edge in the job marketplace. This is just another example of getting paid to help others, while learning information that will come in handy down the road.

Benefits of Earning While Learning

"Earning while learning provides the student with both financial assistance to help meet college expenses and practical experience which may lead to enhanced opportunities for employment after college graduation" (Luzzo, 1996)

In summary, there are many benefits to working on-campus while you're enrolled as a full-time student.

- **Pay the Tuition Tab.** Student employment is an effective means of paying for college while building your resume. Even if the experience is not related to your field of study, the self-confidence you develop and the connections you make will prove valuable in the future.

- **Save on Taxes.** A recent IRS ruling exempts students who work part-time at their college or university (20 hours per week or less) from paying social security/medicare taxes! These taxes, equal to 7.65 percent of wages, must be paid if you work off-campus at part-time job unrelated to the college or university. Uncle Sam's gift results in more money for you to put towards college expenses, or those CDs and movie tickets!

- **Cut Through the Red Tape.** Working in offices on campus can open doors and shed light on the bureaucratic channels inherent in any size college or university.

- **Test the Waters.** Finally, working while enrolled lets you try out different work settings, tasks and styles. This "reality test" lets you experience the world of work without losing the "ivory tower" benefits of full-time student status.

Much research points to the fact that college work experiences are directly related to successful employment after graduation. Students who have worked in different settings with different people are simply better prepared for their first "real" job, than their counterparts who did not have such experiences. This research is backed up by comments from employers when they come to campus to recruit seniors for jobs after graduation.

Site Seeing

The Student Guide to Financial Aid

http://www.ed.gov/prog_info/SFA/StudentGuide

Provides information on loans, grants, and work-study. Includes links to the Free Application for Federal Student Aid (FAFSA), as well as other programs and applications.

FinAid: The Financial Aid Information Page
http://www.finaid.org

Sponsored by the National Association of Student Financial Aid Administrators, this site guides you through the maze of financial information in cyberspace.

Print References

Luzzo, D.A. (1996). "Career decision-making benefits of college student employment." *Student Employment: Linking College and the Workplace.* (Kincaid, R. ed.) Monograph series 23, National Resource Center for the Freshmen Year Experience and Students in Transition. University of South Carolina, Columbia, SC.

Mulugetta, Y. and Chavez, D. (1996). "National student employment survey: Why students choose to work and their perceptions of the academic year work experience." *Student Employment: Linking College and the Workplace.* (Kincaid, R. ed.) Monograph series 23, National Resource Center for the Freshmen Year Experience and Students in Transition. University of South Carolina, Columbia, SC.

Wilkie, C. and Jones, M. (1996). "Academic benefits of on-campus employment to first year developmental education students."*Student Employment: Linking College and the Workplace.* (Kincaid, R. ed.) Monograph series 23, National Resource Center for the Freshmen Year Experience and Students in Transition. University of South Carolina, Columbia, SC.

CHAPTER 5

■ ■ ■ ■ ■ ■ ■ ■ ■ ■ ■ ■ ■ ■ ■ ■ ■ ■

LEADERSHIP ACTIVITIES AND CAMPUS INVOLVEMENT

*"It is time for a new generation of leadership to cope
with new problems and new opportunities.
For there is a new world to be won."*

—John F. Kennedy

Do you have what it takes to be a campus leader? Of course you do!
Leaders emerge over time as a result of how they tackle challenges and
interact with other people. Everyone, regardless of their experiences, has
the potential to be a leader.

Get Involved

The best way to develop your leadership potential is to get involved at
your college or university. And don't think you must be president or chair of
an organization to be a leader; members of all types of groups can just as
easily take on a leadership role.

College is about more than classes, exams, and books. It's also a time to
discover yourself, and try new things. Student development experts believe
that what goes on outside the classroom is just as important as what
students learn inside the classroom. For this reason, you should use the
same care in designing your "activities curriculum" as your academic one.

Believe it or not, your college years will go by quickly. And they will be
much more memorable if you make the effort to get out and make a
difference. Not only will you feel a sense of accomplishment, but you
inadvertently contribute to your career and personal development. This
chapter explores how involvement in campus and leadership activities

contributes to your college education. It also describes how on- and off-campus activities sharpen your resume, and enhance your employability when the time comes (gasp!) to find a job.

Case Study

Isabella is a new student at a small liberal arts college in New Jersey. She wants to major in French, although she's unsure about where that will lead her in the future. She also has an interest in the social sciences, and will probably minor in sociology or psychology. Feeling a little lonely and homesick during her first semester, Isabella hoped to find an activity to occupy her time. After class, she walked over to the campus activities office and asked for a list of student groups. To her surprise, her college had an active French Club! She attended the club's weekly meeting and learned she had a lot in common with other group members and the group leaders. Ultimately, she became an active member in the organization, and participated in many cultural, educational, and career related activities. She was able to take trips with the group to Montreal, Canada, and each group member took turns hosting cultural pot-luck dinners.

In this example, Isabella felt a need to be involved on campus. She took the initiative to seek out the possibilities, and found the organization that fit her needs. Isabella was able to meet people who shared her interests, and began to develop a new network of friends. So much for being homesick!

Types of Campus Activities

The rest of this chapter explores different types of campus activities, and suggests how they can benefit you—personally, and professionally— during and after your college years.. As you will see, there is truly something for everyone.

Academic-Oriented

Organizations such as the French Club—which focus on a shared academic interest or department-related topic—also have a tendency to sponsor career-related programs to help members find jobs in that field. These programs help focus members on career goals, and enlighten students on the possibilities within a given major. Isabella, for example, doesn't know what she will do when she graduates with a major in French. But if the club's president invites a representative from the career center to speak about career options, Isabella would soon discover that a French major may choose to be a translator for a government office or international agency. Or, she could work abroad for a multinational organization in need of bilingual individuals.

While opening Isabella's eyes to future job prospects, involvement with the French Club may also help fortify her employability. When the opportunity arises to take a leadership role in club activities, Isabella can chair a committee, and ultimately even become president of the organization. She can thus practice her leadership skills and prepare herself for a future career where she may need to lead a team of co-workers.

Academic departments may also sponsor honor fraternities. Beta Alpha Psi, for instance, is a national co-ed accounting fraternity that keeps its members on track in planning for their careers throughout their undergraduate years. The possibilities and opportunities are endless but they all start with identifying your interests, then getting and staying involved.

Student Government

One of the most visible areas of leadership is participation in student government. This option is immediately attractive for individuals interested in politics, but equally beneficial for students interested in other areas. Student government organizations may, for example, have senators responsible for environmental issues or recycling, technology, health and wellness, and a number of other issues. Students do not have to be political science or criminal justice majors to benefit. At many universities, the board of trustees sets aside funding for all students groups, and allows the student government to divvy up the pie. This budgetary and managerial process is educational for students in any major.

Residence Hall Associations

Residence Hall Associations are another form of student government, serving the needs of students living in university-run housing. These organizations thrive under the leadership of student members interested in financial and political issues, programming, development, and management.

Case Study

Lucas, a finance major at Northern U., began college with a drive to be as actively involved in campus life as possible. He attended each weekly hall government meeting, and was elected to represent his residence hall in the campus-wide Residence Hall Association (RHA). With each passing year, Lucas increased his leadership activity with RHA, culminating with his election as Vice President during his senior year. In this role, he coordinated meetings, co-managed the annual budget, helped develop programs, and brainstormed the future role of the organization on that campus. Upon graduation, Lucas applied and was selected for a position as account manager at a financial planning company in New York City. His future supervisor cited his proven leadership abilities and fiscal management experience as top reasons for his selection.

In this case study, Lucas became involved in campus life to develop personally and professionally. He found a niche in an organization which interested him, while pursuing activities he knew would help him in his job search. His skills in managing, programming, developing, and budgeting truly set him apart from other students. Lucas accentuated his leadership involvement with real-life skills and responsibilities which prepared him well for life after college.

Service-to-School

Students who live off-campus are typically not included in Residence Hall Associations, however, they can get involved with powerhouse committees like the campus programming council which decides how to allocate the campus programming budget. At most schools, all types of students—graduate, undergraduate, and from all majors—work together on this effort. Student leaders in this area choose educational, social, and cultural events for the campus, and determine campus needs through direct contact with student "constituents."

Other service-to-school leadership positions include the following:

• A mentor for incoming freshmen
• The student liaison to your college's board of trustees
• The student liaison to your college's dining services committee
• A health and wellness peer educator
• An academic peer advisor
• A career counseling peer advisor

All of these service-to school activities let you volunteer your time to improve your college and the lives of your classmates.

Student Tour Guide

Being a student tour guide is one of the most popular ways to become active on campus. It involves much more than simply learning to walk backwards and talk at the same time. You learn about the history and culture of a college or university, and develop relationships with visiting families. You build wonderful presentation and communication skills, and learn to work well with other people. Tangible benefits differ from school to school, but may include priority class registration, social events and food, and even a small stipend.

Hobby-Related

Joining activities and groups with a specific focus is a good way to meet other people with similar interests, while gaining experience in a given area.

If, for example, you are interested in finance, you may join the Amateur Investors Club. You play a "mock" stock market with your peers, and the school may even provide limited funds for you to invest. Students studying film might join the Classic Film-Watcher's Society. And, bridge players can hone their tournament strategies 24-hours a day.

Even if your hobby doesn't relate to your major or career goals, you will still gain useful team-building and management skills—and show future employers that you can balance both work and leisure activities.

Campus Media

Aspiring journalists may choose to work at the school paper. Or perhaps you are interested in mass communications and want to spend some time at the campus television or radio station. English majors may find an outlet for creativity with the university's literary magazine, and gain published clips for use after graduation. In fields like these, where prior published or broadcast work is truly the litmus test for employment, campus involvement is a must. These activities will provide you with opportunities to help build skills and contribute to your classmates awareness and entertainment.

Religious/Belief Oriented

Some students pursue religious or belief-oriented activities when they arrive on campus. True, most students joining the Buddhist Student Society or the Campus Society Against Meat Eating are not doing so to advance their careers. However, in addition to the skills that all leadership activities teach, religious and belief-oriented groups frequently involve training in counseling, activism, and dealing with diversity. Students who accept leadership positions in such groups are also called upon to be representatives of, and advocates for, their belief systems. Does the University routinely hold exams (or other activities) on Saturdays when devout Jews are not able to participate due to the Sabbath? Well if you are chair of the Student Association for Conservative Judaism, you best brush up on your negotiating skills, because it may be your job to get those exams moved. Once you've tackled that, salary negotiations may not seem so scary!

Cultural Activities

Like religious and belief-oriented activities, cultural groups sometimes involve advocacy work. You may join The Black People's Union to stay tied to your own culture while in college, attend readings of local African-American poets, and help plan the BPU Block Party. You may not have been raised knowing much about your culture, but join the Campus Italian Sisterhood to learn more, and end up hosting a pot-luck dinner with members of many other cultural groups. You might also join a cultural group to learn about the traditions of others. Think about attending a meeting of the Filipino Cultural Coalition or the Turkish Student Society. Delving into cultural activities, you will not only learn about yourself, but you will develop an affinity and understanding for the cultures of others.

Community Service Activities

Certainly the best benefit of service is the help you give to others. But community service time is also looked upon quite favorably by today's employers. Perhaps you will volunteer at a local soup kitchen or at an area homeless shelter. Also, almost every career interest lends itself to service activities. For example, if you have an interest in education or child development you might sign up to be a Big Brother/Big Sister for a neighborhood child or volunteer to tutor at a local school. Combine the personal satisfaction and career experience you get from volunteerism with the good deeds it accomplishes, and you have a recipe every student should include in his or her campus diet.

Athletic Pursuits

If you are a future Hall of Famer, by all means go for it! But even if you aren't, intramural and club sports provide a great outlet for stress, and an opportunity to make friends. Don't limit yourself to traditional sports— organize your dorm and compete in the ultimate frisbee club's campus-wide tournament. Even non-athletes can participate in sports—most teams play against other schools, so the team manager gets great experience planning excursions and budgeting.

Sports activities also build teamwork, discipline and endurance; skills which are essential to the workplace.

Greek Letter Organizations

Hazing, beer guzzling, and falling grades; these are the images that spring to many parents minds when you mention fraternities and sororities. If you learn to balance social and academic commitments, however, Greek letter organizations have much to offer. In addition to camaraderie and support, your sorority/fraternity will monitor your grade point average (most have GPA requirements, and put you on probation should you fall below it), schedule study groups, hold elections, and require service activities. And fraternities and sororities offer their members an invaluable network of alumni in various careers across the country, through which to advance their careers.

Benefits of Leadership and Activities

Participating in a variety of activities can build leadership skills, enhance your self confidence and help you make new friends. This participation also gives you the chance to:

- Create a team environment and build a community
- Provide constructive feedback and manage organizational conflict
- Provide and participate in opportunities promoting cultural pluralism and diversity
- Participate effectively in group decision-making
- Sharpen interpersonal and group communication skills
- Sharpen management skills (e.g. managing finances, developing programs, etc.)
- Think ethically and critically
- Make individual decisions
- Enhance visionary thinking by developing shared visions, setting goals, taking risks

Even if you participate in just a few activities during your college years, those experiences will influence who you are and how attractive you will be to employers when looking for a job after graduation. The important thing to mention here is *quality*, not *quantity*. People aren't expecting you to run a marathon of activities and programs; but you should be involved and committed to groups you truly enjoy working with. If you do, you will be certain to reap the rewards down the line.

Site Seeing

The Student Leader Newsletter
http://www.studentleader.com

Newsletter for student leaders. Provides great career information as well.

Emerging Leaders
http://www.emergingleader.com

Great site dedicated to leadership ideals, and "lessons learned." Archive of articles on topics such as self-leadership, communication, and service among others.

Academy of Leadership

http://www.leadernet.org

Comprehensive site including a global network of leaders contributing to a forum of debate and discussion. Also serves as a clearinghouse for personal and professional development opportunities.

Leader Values

http://www.leader-values.com

Information on past great leaders, as well as a forum to read about individual leadership experiences. Slide presentations on leadership issues posted on a regular basis.

Print References

"Leadership programs from entry to graduation." (March, 1999) Workshop conducted at the meeting of the National Association of Student Personnel Administrators, New Orleans, LA.

*"If we believed in walking down life's beaten path...
we would seldom make any tracks of our own."*

—Victor McGuire

CHAPTER 6

■■■■■■■■■■■■■■■■■■■

VOLUNTEERING AND
SERVICE LEARNING

"Service is the rent you pay for room on this earth."

—Shirley Chisholm

Do you plan to bring your conscience to campus along with your clothes, computer, and stereo? Volunteer work and "service learning" opportunities abound on and around most colleges. If you volunteered your time and energy for a cause in high school, you already have a keen understanding of the role you can play in meeting the needs in our society for food, shelter, education, health, justice, peace and safety.

If you are new to volunteer work, your college years will provide many avenues to express your values, help others and impact your corner of your world.

Case Study ════════════════════════════════

Since Jessica, a college freshman, had always enjoyed working with children, when she arrived on campus she signed up as a volunteer tutor through her college's Community Services Center. She was matched with twelve-year-old Shaniqua, who was at risk of not finishing middle school. Jessica's tutee was transported to campus with ten other children twice each week for a two-hour after-school help session with her reading and math. Jessica quickly discovered that Shaniqua's problems were related more to her low self-esteem than to her academic deficits. So, in addition to helping her with reading and math, Jessica thought up ways to make Shaniqua feel good about herself. Over time, Jessica watched her student blossom from a shy, withdrawn child to an articulate, friendly young woman with improved study habits and a zest for learning.

Working with Shaniqua did take up a lot of Jessica's time, but she had the satisfaction of making a difference in the life of a child, applying some of the theoretical prin- ciples she was learning in her psychology courses, and learning a lot about herself. Jessica felt that her effort was well rewarded and enhanced her college experi- ence.

On campus, you'll hear "volunteer work," "community service" and "service-learning" all used to describe ways of contributing to the well-being of the world around you. Volunteer work and community service usually refer to self-initiated out-of-class experiences which may take place on a regular, limited or one-time-only basis. To learn about opportunities, visit your college's community services office, the student activities office, the career services center, or volunteer fairs. You'll find a multitude of sites where socially-responsible students can help meet community needs.

The shelves of the career resource center or main library also house directories of local, regional, and national volunteer opportunities. Local United Way and non-profit agency directories are chock-full of community agencies which depend on volunteers to carry out their mission. There are also numerous Web sites which provide a clearinghouse for volunteer possibilities. You'll find their addresses in the Resource section of this chapter.

Service Learning

Service Learning was defined by the *1990 National and Community Service Act* as a method "under which students learn and develop through active participation in thoughtfully organized service experiences that meet actual community needs and that are coordinated in collaboration with the school and community." That is, service learning typically integrates students' volunteer work with credit-bearing academic programs—usually in the form of seminars or workshops—which focus on discussion and reflection on what has taken place at the volunteer site, addressing problems and providing feedback. Keeping a log or journal of your experiences, including observations and commentary about people and situations you encounter at your site, is a common service–learning program assignment. There may also be term papers to write and projects to complete. Grades are usually based on supervisor's evaluation and classroom attendance, participation, and projects.

Whether you choose to volunteer in the traditional manner or through a service-learning program, your first step is to figure out what volunteer role will best fit your personality, your tolerance for stress, your skills, your interests...and your schedule! The following descriptions have been adapted from *Volunteer America*.

Direct Service Volunteering

Work with people one-on-one or in small group.

Examples: crisis hotline staffer, visitor to a nursing home, Big Brother to a child from a single parent home, tutor for mentally challenged teenager, activities assistant at a senior center, etc.

Indirect Service Volunteering

Provide behind-the-scenes assistance so that direct service can take place.

Examples: typing letters, stuffing envelopes, making reminder calls for a fundraising event or special program.

Administrative Volunteering

Lend your support to a cause by helping with administrative tasks.

Examples: background research; writing and editing newsletters and brochures; assisting in the planning, coordinating, and carrying out of community, recreational and fundraising events.

Direct Action or Advocacy Volunteering

Organize, educate others, and work for change in services and systems. *Examples: lobbying for prison reform, animal rights, improved services for the elderly; participating in political campaigns; registering voters before election day, etc.*

Volunteer Opportunities

Next, decide where you want to volunteer your time and energy. There is no shortage of worthy causes that cry out for your attention:

- AIDs advocacy organizations
- Day care centers
- Drug prevention programs
- Handicapped groups (special Olympics, schools for the deaf)
- Homeless people (housing, literacy, employment)
- Homebound elderly
- Hospitals
- Juvenile justice
- Police departments (neighborhood watch, victim assistance)
- Prisons
- Recreation programs (teen centers, sports, scouting)
- Schools (wellness programs, dropout prevention, tutoring)
- U.S. Senators' or members of the House of Representatives' offices

Advantages of Volunteering

- Provides the opportunity to exercise your conscience and civic responsibilities and build lifetime habits of the heart.
- Builds a network of community contacts.
- Allows the flexibility to schedule your volunteer efforts so as not to disrupt academic work.
- Leads to information about options for post-graduate study.
- Allows you to learn about career possibilities.
- Forges links between classroom work and real-world situations.
- Encourages meaningful relationships with fellow-students, supervisors, and community members.

* Builds emotional comfort, self-confidence, and autonomy in interpersonal situations.
* Hones skills that relate to job situations.
* Broadens your world by increasing the range of places and people you know about and with whom you feel a connection.
* Enhances academic development.

Disadvantages of Volunteering

* May lead to frustration and disillusionment if societal problems don't quickly yield to individual efforts.
* Does not provide financial help to defray college expenses.
* Can challenge student priorities since it can be harder to cancel your shift at the battered woman's shelter than to turn down your shift at the cafeteria come exam time.

Site Seeing

Action Without Borders
http://www.idealist.org

Search a database of 16,000 nonprofit organizations by programs, country, or organizational name. A global clearinghouse of nonprofit and voluntary resources.

Impact On-Line
http://www.impactonline.org

Impact Online is a nonprofit organization dedicated to helping people get involved in their community.

National Society for Experiential Education
http://www.nsee.org

VolunteerMatch
http://www.volunteermatch.com

In partnership with thousands of local nonprofit organizations VolunteerMatch has built a comprehensive and up-to-date database of volunteer opportunities. You can search thousands of volunteer opportunities by zip code, category and date.

The World of Service and Volunteering
http://www.servenet.org

Stories about "service heroes" and service initiatives as well as a database of opportunities, a weekly news service, and volunteer of the month awards.

Volunteer Work Experience Program
http://www.sdc.uwo.cal/int/volunteer.html

A sample volunteer program run by the University of Western Ontario.

Print References

Journal of College Student Development, "How Undergraduates are affected by Service Participation," Alexander Astin and Linda Sax, May/June 1998.

Volunteer U.S.A., Andrew Carroll, Fawcett Columbine, 1991.

The Call of Service, Robert Coles, Houghton Miflin Company, 1993.

Good Works: A Guide to Careers in Social Change, Edited by Donna Colvin, Barricade Books, NY, 1994.

Volunteer America: A Comprehensive National Guide to Opportunities for Service, Training and Work Experience, edited by Harriet Clyde Kipps, Ferguson Publishing Co., 1997.

The Quickening of America, Frances Moore Lappe and Paul Martin duBois, Jossey-Bass, Inc., 1994.

Common Fire: Lives of Commitment in a Complex World, Laurent and Sharon Parks, Beacon Press, 1996.

Service Matters: Engaging Higher Education in the Renewal of America's Communities, edited by Michael Rothman, Campus Contact, 1998.

The National Directory of Children, Youth and Families Services 1998-99, Penny K. Spencer, 1998.

Making a Difference College Guide, Miriam Weinstein, The Princeton Review, Random House, 1996.

*"There is a destiny that makes us brothers and sisters.
None goes his way alone. What we send into the lives of others
comes back into our own."*

—Edwin Markham

CHAPTER 7

································

COOPERATIVE EDUCATION

*"One must learn by doing the thing; for though you think
you know it you have not certainty until you try."*

—Sophocles

Nearly one thousand college campuses nationwide list cooperative
education programs among their offerings. Derived from a relationship of
cooperation between industry and academia, "learn and earn" programs
place students in field assignments related to their academic and career
goals. Students provide productive work to their employing organization
and, in most cases, are paid for their work and receive college credit as well
as a notation on their transcript.

Case Study

*Emily, an accounting major, had worked as a cashier and bank
teller during her summer vacations. By her junior year at
college, she was pretty sure she wanted to pursue corporate
accounting but needed experience in the field to build her skills
and to help her make an informed decision about her future
career. The accounting department at Emily's college advertised
a co-op program which listed several corporate accounting field
placements in its data base. Doing a co-op meant Emily would
be at a work site far from campus from July to December, paid
between twelve and fifteen dollars per hour, and helped with
finding temporary housing. During her co-op, she would be
introduced to and trained in corporate accounting and given the
chance to make professional contacts in the field. The downside*

was that her graduation date would have to be delayed for one semester. Emily's roommates were surprised that she was gutsy enough to leave the security of campus life for a temporary position forty miles away at a major company, but they knew students who did co-op had a definite edge over the competition when it came to finding full-time employment after graduation.

Some colleges, known as "co-op schools," have mandatory cooperative education placements. In these schools, degree requirements include periods of supervised work experience at approved business or industrial sites.

Other colleges, like Emily's, have co-op programs as an optional departmental offering. Depending on the college, co-op programs may be defined in very different ways. On some campuses, co-ops are similar to internships, on other campuses they are distinctively different. Thoroughly reading college catalogues, and asking the right questions of admission personnel should clarify the co-op program at specific colleges.

According to the Cooperative Education Association, there are more than 117,000 official co-op placement sites throughout the United States. Most co-op sites are for- profit organizations. For example, Bell Atlantic, Bristol-

Meyers, Coca-Cola, Dupont, Exxon, IBM, Merck, Merrill Lynch, Xerox and other Fortune 500 companies are all active co-op employers. Many companies use their co-op programs to train and recruit future full-time employees. A large number of nonprofit organizations and governmental agencies also offer co-op opportunities to college students.

Co-op programs are usually structured into two types of work plans. The alternating plan allows college students to alternate semesters of full-time course work with six month co-op work experiences. The parallel program allows students to work part-time while attending classes and graduating on-schedule.

The *Directory of College Cooperative Education Programs,* available from the American Council on Education, outlines and profiles cooperative education programs at four hundred sixty institutions of higher learning. You can view an even larger list of colleges that offer co-op by clicking on the Cooperative Education Association's Web page (see Web Resources below).

Advantages of Co-op

- Helps confirm or reject career possibilities by trying a career on for size.
- Develops professional skills and contacts.
- Builds confidence, competency and self-esteem.
- Enhances classroom learning by integrating academic curriculum and real world work-related problems.
- Provides a competitive edge when seeking employment after graduation.
- Helps defray college costs.

Disadvantages of Co-op

- May delay graduation by one or more semesters.
- May limit time that might be spent on academic electives and eclectic campus activities.
- May cause premature focus on one field without taking the time to explore other options.

Site Seeing

The World Association for Cooperative Education
http://dac.neu.edu/wace

Cooperative Education Network
http://www.co-op.uc.edu/home

The Cooperative Education Association,
http://www.ceainc.org

Print References

The Center for Cooperative Education, Northeastern University, 360 Huntington Avenue, Boston, MA 02115.

The Directory of College Cooperative Education Programs, edited by Polly Hutcheson, Available from the American Council on Education, Oryx Press Series on Higher Education, Phoenix, AZ (1998).

CHAPTER 8

■■■■■■■■■■■■■■■■■■

INTERNSHIPS

*"The most profound question next to "Who am I" is
"What do I want to do." And interestingly enough, both of
these questions become clear only by experimentation.
There is no way to know beforehand."*

—Adele Scheele

Have you ever purchased a new pair of shoes without trying them on first? Or, bought a new car without going for a test drive? If you are like most people, the answer to both of these questions is "no." So why, then, would you pursue a career without ever experiencing it first-hand? This is where an internship can be of great value! More and more employers are reporting how important it is for college graduates to have internship experiences. But internships do more than just help you get your foot in the door of that perfect job after graduation, they also help you:

1. Develop into a well-rounded person.

2. Enhance your employability by sharpening your interpersonal communications skills, exposing you to office politics, and teaching you to work well with others.

3. Establish a good rapport with your supervisor, which can soon turn into a mentoring relationship.

4. Establish valuable contacts so even if you do not want to work at that organization, or even in that field, you can still use your new connections for references and networking purposes.

In this chapter, we will define the term "internship," discuss the value of internships, help you learn how to find the right internship, and give you suggestions to help you make the most of your internship experience.

Case Study

Jeremy is a first semester sophomore at Woodbridge College. Although still undecided about his major and career, Jeremy has always enjoyed creative writing. He has done well in English, and prefers writing essays to taking multiple-choice tests. Jeremy thinks he may want to major in Public Relations, Journalism, or English, but wants to have a "real-life" experience before making the choice. He decides to intern at a small public relations firm. While there, Jeremy has the opportunity to dabble in different areas of PR: from writing, to media database management, to making phone pitches to local editors and reporters. He soon realized, however, that his real joy continued to be writing. At the conclusion of his semester, Jeremy decided to major in creative writing, and saw a future for himself in writing press releases or news stories.

In this case, Jeremy knew his interests. He also seemed to be well aware of his talents. He needed to participate in this internship experience to reinforce his confidence in his abilities, and get some career direction. The experience allowed him to get his feet wet, and develop real-world skills which will surely help him build his career.

Many students begin their freshmen year knowing exactly what they want to major in, or even exactly which career they wish to pursue. That's perfectly fine! But many students are not only undecided, they may even be confused about the choices available to them. This is where the services at your college or university can help. Counselors are trained to help you make career-related choices. Your first step is to seek out those services; make some phone calls, check the department's Web site, and most importantly, sign up for an advising appointment. Thirty minutes out of your day can make the difference between a confused random choice and an informed career decision.

Sometimes, Internships can make clear what you don't necessarily want in a career. Take for example, Case Study 2:

Case Study

Katherine is a freshman at a large urban university. She began college thinking about a career in politics. During her second semester, a career counselor at her University recommended that Katherine learn more about politics by spending time at an internship. After consulting the University Career Center for available internships, she decided to intern at a local legislator's office. Throughout her experience, Katherine enjoyed working with the media and the press, while she was bored by the politics and fundraising. While Katherine had a successful and enjoyable experience in the end, she realized she had other strengths and interests, and perhaps politics was not exactly the right fit for her.

Many students use internships to get experience in certain fields; others use them to explore interests, and, as a result, determine what careers they *don't* want to pursue. In this example, Katherine entered college knowing she liked politics. Yet after gaining some real-life experience, she realized this was not a field for her. The internship was not, however, a waste of time—it awakened her interest in media relations and communications, allowing her to re-focus her career goals.

Trying Careers on for Size

Let's explore this idea another way. If, for example, you are undecided about your college major, internships can help guide you toward a career direction. Thinking back to Chapter 3 ("Career Assessment"), you will remember that choosing a field has much to do with your *interests*. (If you completed the assessment worksheets in Chapter 3, read on. Otherwise, go back and spend some time with these tools. Not only will they help you with this chapter, they will allow you to learn more about yourself!) Take a quick look at what you listed as some of your interests. How you can apply those interests to an internship?

Example One

Let's say you indicated an interest in helping others. Perhaps you can relate that interest to an internship at a senior center or nursing home. After the first week or two, you may realize you enjoy working with older people. That can equate to an Individual and Family Studies major, or another related human services type major.

Example Two

Let's say you love animals. At first glance, you may think "what can I possibly do that would relate to my love of animals?" Firstly, don't shoot the idea down just because you aren't strong in the sciences. Perhaps you can be a photographer for animal-related magazines like *National Geographic* or *Cat Fancy*. Or, perhaps you can intern in the educational division of the local aquarium or zoo, helping teach students and visiting groups about the animal world. As you can see, it's not necessary to be a scientist to work with animals.

Example Three

Let's say you are interested in sports. You acknowledge, however, that you aren't the next Michael Jordan or Mia Hamm. Remember—you don't have to be a sports superstar! You can intern at a local radio or television station assisting in their sports broadcasting division. Or, you may have an interest in the health side of sports, and thus intern in an organization which provides athletic training and sports medicine to athletes.

The possibilities are endless—you just have to take some time to relate your interests to potential internships, which may lead to a job you will love!

What Are My Options?

OK—we've convinced you that interning is an important tool in the construction of your "second curriculum." Now, we'll talk about some of the options you face when choosing to participate in an internship. Use the following questions to help you focus:

1. When do you want to intern? Should you look for internship positions over the summer months or winter session (if applicable), or can you intern during the academic year? Answering this question will help you narrow the options and decide on the right position.

2. Where do you want to focus your search? Will you be looking for positions nationally? locally? back home so you can live with your parents? The answer to this question will help you determine appropriate internship search strategies (later in this chapter).

3. What are your expectations about being paid? Some of the most valuable internships are unpaid, so don't limit yourself. Instead, consider everything about the position—the career experience you'll be getting, the contacts you will make, and the possibility of a job offer after you graduate. When you compare these benefits, the experience can outweigh the money. And remember, you can always combine a part-time internship with a part-time job (especially over the summer), to help alleviate any financial burden.

4. Do you hope to receive academic credit for your internship experience? Many organizations that host student interns (especially those that don't pay), require students to receive some form of academic credit from their home institution. In their opinion, this adds to the educational component of the experience. Make sure you understand those stipulations before applying for positions, and decide for yourself if you are interested in those academic credits. Most institutions offer a for-credit experiential education or internship class. Even colleges that don't offer a credit class will probably allow students to register for an independent study course so they can obtain credits for the experience. Discover your options, and weigh the positives and negatives associated with obtaining credit.

5. What type of internship environment appeals to you? Will you be happier at a small company, or large institution? Would you rather intern for an organization with a large, established internship program, or are you willing to be the only intern in the office?

Finding an Internship

Well, now that we've talked about how important interning is to your career development, lets turn our discussion towards the meatier subject—how to go about finding the perfect internship experience for you. The task can seem overwhelming, but like anything else, it becomes more manageable when you break it down bit by bit.

Using the Career Center

Most students begin their search in the career library at their campus Career Services Center. This office will have a number of very helpful resources to assist you in the search process, even if you are completely undecided about your field of interest.

Most campus career centers devote a section of their libraries to internships. First, consult the binders containing information on local (and national) internship positions. These binders, with their frequently-updated listings, will prove invaluable, especially if your search is focused on the immediate geographic area of your college. Second, consult some of the national internship books, such as those published by Peterson's or Kaplan. These books list internships in a directory format, usually with cross-referenced indexes in the back. The guides will also give you some strategies and hints about applying for the internships listed.

And be sure to make friends with the career librarian or desk assistant—they work with this literature every day and can point you in the right direction if you are feeling lost or confused.

Using the Internet

The Internet is becoming another very popular resource for the internship search. Most students find it especially useful when trying to locate a position outside of their current residential area. Each year, there are more and more sites with internship listings, and advice for students who want to maximize their internship experience. You should certainly check out these sites, but don't rely on them exclusively. The Internet should be just another tool in your career construction plan.

Using "People Resources"

Another successful method of finding that great internship is to use the "people resources" available to you. Faculty, staff, and family members can prove valuable in any type of "job" hunt. Faculty may have contacts in their fields, and may know of openings before the campus career center is informed. Family members may have openings in their organizations, or have friends in a field that may interest you. The bottom line here is be sure to let as many people as possible know you are looking for an internship. You would be surprised at how fast word travels, and how advantageous those relationships can be to your status as a potential intern! You've now completed Networking 101.

Do Some Research

If, after using all these resources, you still haven't found an internship that appeals to you, then it's time to get your hands dirty and do some research. You may want to work backwards—i.e., start with a list of companies that interest you, and determine if they have an internship program. Consult the campus career center's library, and be sure to look through phone books and industry directories to find the names and numbers of organizations you wish to pursue. Check out their Web sites, and make phone calls to their human resource offices. Ask to speak to the person in charge of their internship program, and if no one there has that title, ask to speak with the person in charge of college recruiting and hiring. Even if they don't have an annual "internship program," offer to volunteer some time and become their very first intern! Be persistent, but don't become a pest. Respect the value of their time. If they aren't returning your second and third phone calls, move on to another organization. But don't let a few failed attempts detract you from your goal—the right internship experience is out there waiting for you!

Ready, Set, Go!

So you've found the perfect internship experience. It's in the field you want, in the geographic area you want, and you'll be performing the day-to-day activities that will build up your resume. Now what? First things first....congratulate yourself on a "job search" well done! Meanwhile, send thank-you notes and letters of regret to any internship offers you've turned down. It's important to be as professional as possible: You never know if the person who interviewed you for a position you didn't take will be your future boss elsewhere!

The next step is an important one. You should ask your campus career center for a sample "learning contract." This short form acts as an "employment contract" with your internship site supervisor. In this contract, you should specify your duties, your hours, and the terms of your internship. Not that you don't trust your sponsor, but it's always better to get these details down on paper, so you can refer to them later. You also don't want any surprises springing up down the road. You should always know what duties you will be performing, as well as your supervisor's expectations. This will ensure a positive experience for everyone involved, and will help you evaluate your experience against the goals you have set for yourself.

Finally, go off and knock 'em dead! Be sure to impress the folks you work with, as you may be asking them for recommendations down the road. Have a good experience, but remember; you are still a student. No one is expecting you to climb the corporate ladder in one semester!

Site Seeing

Jobtrak Summer Jobs and Internships
http://www.jobtrak.com

Provides a database searchable by field and region. National and local internship programs are included.

Catapult Summer Jobs and Internships
http://www.jobweb.org/catapult/jintern.htm

Searchable directories to listings and organizational profiles.

Intern-NET
http://www.vicon.net/~internnet

Powerful site with a searchable database listing internships by region or field. Also provides online in-depth career library.

Internship Programs
http://www.internshipprograms.com

National Internship Sites
http://www.wm.edu/csrv/career/stualum/jintern.html

Comprehensive online listing of internships in a variety of geographic and specialty areas.

Print References

Internships, Sara Dulaney Gilbert, Macmillan, 1995.

The National Directory of Internships, Gila Gulati and Nancy Bailey. *National Society for Internships and Experiential Education*, 1999.

America's Top 100 Internships, Mark Oldman and Samer Hamaden, Willard Books, 1996.

Internship Success, Marianne Green, VGM Career Horizons, 1997.

The Peterson's Guide to Internships, Peterson's, 1999.

InternAmerica, 105 Chestnut St., Suite 34, Needham, MA 02192.

CHAPTER 9

■■■■■■■■■■■■■■■■■■■■■

MAKING THE MOST OF
YOUR ELECTIVES

"I never let my schooling interfere with my education."

—Mark Twain

Whatever your major, interests, goals or career path, there are several key classes which will broaden and deepen your skills and bolster your chances of success as an undergraduate and beyond. Some majors already include one or more of these helpful courses, but the far-sighted college student will reap the benefits by adding them as electives. Electives, sometimes called "free electives," are classes you freely choose to take; they are not required for your major or degree. They offer you the chance to exercise your curiosity, express your creativity, diversify your background, and develop and practice new skills by exposing you to out-of-major courses.

Case Study

Martel, an anthropology major, took steps early on in his academic career to add "practical" courses to his social sciences major. He eventually wanted a career in human resources, working with recruitment, employee benefits, and affirmative action. Knowing that the connection between his major and his desired occupation wasn't obvious, Martel made sure he chose several elective courses to diversify his background. As a sophomore, he took a computer science course to learn the basics of word processing, spreadsheets, and data bases. During his junior year, Martel polished his Spanish skills by spending a winter term studying in Madrid. Over the summer,

*he took a business class at a college in his hometown to learn
more about the for-profit world. When these electives appeared
on his resume, coupled with a rich array of out-of-class experiences, Jason's varied background and capabilities attracted the
attention of employers in the business world, even though he was
not a business major.*

Key Electives for Career Success

If your college major and group requirements don't include the following
types of courses, make it a point to tackle them during your college career,
possibly during a special session or over the summer. You may not see their
relevance now, but they will definitely pay off for you in the future.

Foreign Language/Study Abroad

If your schedule permits, study and practice a foreign language to the
point where you can carry on a meaningful conversation and comprehend
articles in a foreign language newspaper. In today's global economy,
employers from all fields search for candidates who speak more than one
language. Spanish and Japanese are recognized as especially useful in
today's marketplace.

Study abroad will build your appreciation for and comfort-level with
cultural diversity. Many students set their sights on working internationally
after graduation, but don't take steps to sharpen their foreign language skills
and engage in cross-cultural interactions, limiting their appeal to international employers or American organizations operating overseas.

Business Writing Classes

Written communications skills are repeatedly cited as a top priority for new hires across occupations. Even if business writing seems unrelated to your major, the ability to write and edit succinct reports, memos, business letters, announcements, and proposals will benefit you in whatever job you undertake. Many employers now ask job applicants for writing samples, and your term paper on Shakespeare or modern European history just won't fill the bill. Generally, employers prefer something more practical, like samples drawn from business writing courses.

Sales/Marketing Classes

Learning the how's and why's of sales techniques, sales processes, and customer service has applicability to an array of jobs. Promoting a service or selling a product is an integral part of leadership, community service, and employment. No matter what field you pursue—from politics, to teaching, to medicine, to engineering, to business—you will encounter elements of sales and marketing. If you stop and think about it, applying and interviewing for a job is an exercise in selling yourself!

Oral Communication

Many people say that one of their greatest fears is speaking before a group of people; yet, presentation skills continue to be a critical requirement for many occupations. Even a research scientist, locked away in a laboratory most of the time, must be capable of presenting ideas orally at conferences and professional forums.

Search out an oral communication class so that you can increase your comfort level and fluency when addressing individuals and groups. Enhanced oral communications skills will definitely prove helpful on the job and in your community interactions, on campus as well as off.

Computer Classes

We live in a computer age. Every college graduate of the new millennium needs to be comfortable with personal computers and mainframes, understand and successfully use word processing, spreadsheet, data base management, and desktop publishing software. Employers expect you to be able to utilize e-mail, send attachments, and be a "good driver" on the information superhighway. Constructing your own Web page and displaying your Web page address on your resume will push your resume to the top of an

employer's pile, whatever your educational or vocational objectives may be!
You need not be a computer geek (although most of them are now
zillionaires), but you do need more than a nodding acquaintance with this
critically important technology.

Research

Are you interested in going to graduate or professional school? Research
is a vital part of advanced studies in every field. Undergraduate research
opportunities will equip you with the tools to do your own research as a
junior member of a faculty research team. In most colleges, students have
the chance to share in a professional researcher's work, to learn how to
formulate a significant question and develop a procedure to investigate it,
gather and examine evidence, and evaluate and share results with the
scientific, scholarly, or artistic community.

Advantages to Career-Oriented Electives:

• Adds valuable skills and information to any curriculum.

• Forges a connection between the liberal arts major and a career.

Disadvantages to Career-Oriented Electives:

• Limits the number of other electives that might be chosen.

CHAPTER 10

■■■■■■■■■■■■■■■■■■■■■■

TIME-MANAGEMENT:
YOUR JUGGLING ACT

*"Time is an ally of those who will
seize it and use it to the full."*

—Thomas Edison

Taking full advantage of the second curriculum does not have to mean swamping yourself with more activities than you can possibly handle! Each individual college student must use self-knowledge, time-management skills and common sense to strategically balance academics with other activities.

Though you wish you could "do it all," most students need to pick and choose among the myriad activities college has to offer or they will find themselves over-extended, over-loaded and over-whelmed.

Case Study

Jonathan, a freshman math major, is in trouble. He looks with dismay at the pile of schoolwork on his desk and buries his head in his hands.

In two hours time he has to finish studying for a test and complete an article for his college newspaper. Then he has to attend a meeting of the hiking club across campus.

Jonathan is also well-aware that his application to serve on the college judicial board is due tomorrow and that he has to make good on his promise to collect his dorm's bottles and cans and take them to the re-cycling center no later than 8:00 this evening.

He promised a friend he'd go to his intramural basketball game, and he needs to return a frantic call from an elementary school student he is tutoring. It is very clear to Jonathan that, in an effort to make the most of his college experience, he has bitten off far more than he can chew!

Time Management Tips

The tips in this chapter will help make the second curriculum work *for* rather than *against* you so you don't find yourself in Jonathan's shoes!

Start slowly

Take on one or two extracurricular activities during your freshman year and see how it goes. Everything about college is so new and challenging that first year; you really need to take the time to feel your way. Resist the urge to dive in willy nilly.

Choose quality over quantity

You will learn more and make a greater contribution by sticking with fewer activities over a longer period of time, slowly increasing your level of responsibility and leadership. Superficial and sporadic participation in numerous activities doesn't usually lead to quality experience and skill development.

Leadership, a valued quality in the job market, is honed by chairing a committee, serving as the treasurer of a club, or holding an office in student government—not from claiming membership in many organizations. From a potential employer's view, less can definitely be more!

Combine necessity with quality by selecting second curriculum activities which serve a dual purpose

For example, if you need a part-time job to meet your financial needs, try to land one in a career field of interest to you, even if your responsibilities are fairly mundane. Here's your chance to learn more about potential careers and network with professionals at the same time. Ambitious students have sometimes turned "survival" jobs into exciting internships. It is also possible to obtain credit for internships, easing your course-load and hastening graduation. Are you doing an independent study? Choose a topic that will build your knowledge of a particular career interest.

Consider volunteer work

For the student pressed for time, volunteer work can be personally rewarding as well as an outstanding source of career information and skill enhancement. You can usually set your own volunteer hours, thus scheduling your work around your class schedule and other commitments. Shadowing, extern, and day-on-the-job programs can also provide valuable short-term exposure to jobs of potential interest, when full-blown internships are too time-consuming.

Turn social organizations into opportunities for skill building and career related experience

In addition to taking advantage of a college fraternity's or social club's access to friendships and entertainment, try on the role of events planner, treasurer, membership chair or philanthropy chair.

Build on your career interests

If you already have specific career interests, get involved with related activities—those that will build on and enhance your interests, and "look good" on your resume and graduate school applications:

- **Social Services**—Staff a crisis hot-line; take part in AIDS awareness programming; volunteer for a cause that's near and dear to your heart; do an internship with the department of social services; become a Big Sister; take a service-learning course; become a peer counselor.

- **Politics**—Volunteer for a local representative's campaign; run for office in student government; intern on Capitol Hill during the summer; become part of the model U.N.

- **Publishing**—Become part of the editorial board for your college's literary magazine, yearbook or newspaper; intern with an academic or commercial publishing company; take a summer job proofreading at a magazine.

- **Law**—Join the college's pre-law student association; visit regional and college law school forums; take a summer job as a "runner" for a law firm; intern with the state attorney general's office; participate actively in the college's judiciary board; shadow a lawyer for a day.

- **Engineering**—Take part in special co-op and summer jobs programs for engineers; tutor fellow students; become a teaching assistant for a freshman engineering class.

- **Sales and Marketing**—Work part time for college newspaper selling advertising space; join the student chapter of the American Marketing Association; find a summer job doing focus groups for new products; serve as membership chair for your sorority; intern for a sports team promoting ticket sales; use your winter break to get some retail sales experience.

- **Environment**—Spearhead a campus-wide push for re-cycling; join the environmental issues club; intern for the Nature Conservancy; do a service-learning project educating preschoolers about their environment; write an article for the school newspaper on maintaining an environmentally friendly campus.

- **International**—Become fluent in at least one foreign language; join an international club; do an internship at the International Center on campus; tutor students who are acquiring English as their second language; study abroad; look for a part-time job at the Hispanic community center; live in special language-oriented student housing.

- **Medicine**—Volunteer as a peer counselor at the health center; do a co-op at the emergency room of a local hospital; do a service-learning project at a nursing home; write a series of articles for the college newspaper on health-related problems faced by students; spend a day shadowing the coroner; find a summer job doing research at a pharmaceutical company.

- **Financial Services**—Volunteer to help senior citizens with tax preparation; take a summer job at a bank; serve as treasurer of a club; co-op at an insurance company.

- **Journalism/Media**—Work on your school newspaper or yearbook; intern at a community newspaper or magazine; write copy for an on-line publication; write and edit articles for the swim-team's newsletter; contribute to the campus literary magazine; participate in the campus radio and television stations; intern at a major network in New York City during the summer.

- **Computer Science**—Work part-time at the college computer center's help-desk; take a summer job at a computer store; find a co-op at a major company through campus career services; design an exciting Web page for yourself and others.

- **Art**—Pursue a work-study job at the campus gallery; run an art class at the Boys and Girls Club; intern at the local art museum; design brochures and posters to promote a traveling art exhibit; volunteer at the community arts center; exhibit your art work at juried shows.

As enticing and advantageous as the second curriculum can be, you must honor your academic commitments first. If necessary, look into workshops on time-management or study skills to help you discover and maintain the right balance of co-curricular activities and quality study time. As you begin college, your goal should be to do your best to achieve a distinguished grade point average, coupled with a diverse record of out-of-class accomplishments.

Site Seeing

Time Management Tips
http://www.gmu.edu/gmu/personal/time.html

This list of helpful hints was prepared by the Service for Counseling and Student Development at George Mason University.

Improving Time Management Skills
http://www.smartbiz.com/sbs/arts/bly56.htm

General suggestions on how to set priorities to more effectively manage your time and your life.

CHAPTER 11

■■■■■■■■■■■■■■■■■■■■

DOCUMENTING YOUR EXPERIENCE: RESUMES AND PORTFOLIOS

"A resume is like a sculpture: you keep building—
chipping away here, moving this over there,
trying out another word or phrase or arrangement—
until, Voila!, it works."

—Yana Parker

Everyone needs a resume. In our society, your resume is your "calling card," a dynamic summary of the experiences and training that makes you unique. Resumes, an indispensable tool for the full-time job search, have gained increasing importance for the undergraduate in pursuit of part-time and summer jobs, internships, co-ops, scholarships, and graduate school admissions. If you don't already have a resume, there's no time like the present to create one.

The resume you construct today will only vaguely resemble the one you will eventually prepare for your job search in your final year of college. Your resume is a "living" document which grows and changes as you do. With each passing semester, you should update and reorganize your resume, adding new information about jobs, activities, skills, and training, and subtracting past material which is no longer relevant.

Since there is no one "right" way to compose a resume, over time you may decide to experiment with different fonts, methods of organization and wording. You may also need to prepare a resume specially formatted for scanning into a computer or entering on-line in various computerized data bases. With today's word processing technology, creating and revising your resume is neither difficult nor time-consuming.

Case Study

Denise wanted to act quickly when she read about the perfect summer internship for a fashion merchandising major—interning with Liz Claiborne in New York City. She was taken aback, however, when she learned that a resume was an essential part of the application procedure. Since she had never put a resume together, Denise was forced to do a rush job, sending off a resume that failed to effectively portray her experiences.

College career offices usually offer workshops and seminars on resume writing, as well as helpful advice on formats, word choice, and presentation. Career counselors and peer advisors will critique a rough draft of your resume. For additional help, books on resume writing proliferate on library and bookstore shelves. There are also Web sites which offer tips for the beginning resume writer.

Building Your Resume

Keep these key ideas in mind as you begin to build your first resume or make changes in your current one:

Be brief

A one page resume is almost always long enough to cover the highlights of your academic background, job experiences, activities, and skills. As a mid-career professional, your resume might expand to two pages, but one page is recommended for the undergraduate college student. A longer resume may strike the reader as "puffery"—an attempt to make more of your experience than it really merits.

Be accurate

An error-free resume communicates your attention to detail and organizational skills. Many students have been passed over because they didn't use spell-check, or, because they relied solely on spell-check.

Be proud

Stress your accomplishments. Use action verbs, examples and numbers to create a vivid picture of your achievements. Your resume is not the place for false modesty.

Sample Resumes

Take a look at Tamara Jones' two resumes—constructed four years apart—during her freshman and senior years. The contrast between the two resumes illustrates in a striking way how much Tamara has accomplished during her college years. Her final resume effectively documents the knowledge, experiences, and skills that will make her a viable candidate for a job, admission to graduate or professional school, or a fellowship after graduation. We know that Tamara's future resumes will continue to change in content and style, reflecting additional education and career progress.

In addition to a resume, you might want to assemble a portfolio—a binder or notebook where you collect and display samples of your work. While your resume provides information about your academic background, jobs, activities, and skills, your portfolio contains visual proof of your accomplishments. Use your portfolio to store copies of flyers you designed for your membership campaign, feature articles you wrote for the college newspaper, pictures you took of the walk-a-thon you coordinated for a charitable cause, press releases you wrote at your internship, reports you prepared for your research, etc. A well-organized portfolio, containing clear evidence of your contributions on and off campus, will build your self-confidence, as well as prove a useful tool in your job search.

The method by which you document and present your out-of-class and academic experiences to others is nearly as important as having the experiences in the first place! Your resume is the critical "advertisement" that will draw potential supervisors, coordinators, and employers to you. Your portfolio provides compelling evidence of your skills and abilities.

Start your resume and portfolio early in your college career and keep updating the content. It is extremely hard to start from scratch and produce a winning resume or an effective portfolio on short notice.

Site Seeing

Jobsmart

http://jobsmart.org/tools/resume/yana24/htm

Nationally-known career counselor shares twenty-four of her best resume tips.

Preparing a Resume

http://www.rpi.edu/dept/llc/writecenter/web/test/resume.html

Step-by-step guide to preparing your first resume.

Resume Tutor

http://umn.edu/ohr/ecep/resume

An interactive workbook designed to make resume writing easier and more fun.

Your Resume

http://owl.english.purdue.edu/Files/35.html

A clear, easy-to-follow guide for resume preparation.

Print References

Easy Resume Guide: A Transferable Skills Approach, Barbara J. Bowes, Hushion House, 1999.

101 Tips for a Dynamite Resume, Richard Fein, Impact Publishing Company, 1998.

The Complete Idiot's Guide to the Perfect Resume, Susan Ireland, MacMillan General Reference, 1996.

Cyberspace Resume Kit: How to Make and Launch a Snazzy Online Resume. Mary B. Nemnich, Jist works, 1998.

Resumes for Dummies, Joyce Lain Kennedy, IDG Books Worldwide, 1998.

TAMARA N. JONES
34523@udel.edu

Campus Address	**Permanent Address**
Rodney 233D.	387 Pelliger Avenue
Newark, DE 19716	Wilmington, DE 19708
(302)555-9333	(302) 555-9292

OBJECTIVE
Internship in field related to criminal justice, to gain valuable experience.

EDUCATION
Bachelor of Arts in Criminal Justice, University of Delaware, Newark, DE
(Anticipated Graduation Date: May, 2000)
Enrolled in introductory courses in criminal justice, society
and the law, and abnormal psychology.

High School Diploma, St. Marks High School, Wilmington, DE
(May, 1996) G.P.A. 3.311/4.0

WORK EXPERIENCE
Camp Counselor, Camp Arrowhead, Iron Hill, MD Summer, 1996
* Supervised ten campers between the ages of 6 and 10
* Planned recreational activities
* Directed camp musical production

Bagger, Acme Markets, Wilmington, DE   1995-May, 1996
* Worked 15 hours per week while attending school

Babysitter, The Marshall Family, Wilmington, DE 1993-1995

SKILLS
Word Perfect; three years of Spanish

HONORS AND ACTIVITIES
Pre-Law Student Association	Fall, 1996
National Honor Society	1995-May,1996
Spanish Club	1995-May, 1996
Hosted a foreign exchange student from Panama	1995-August,1996

References Available Upon Request

Senior Year Resume

Tamara N. Jones
657 Lehigh Road Apt. F-11

Local Phone   Newark, DE 19711   **Permanent Phone**
(302) 555-3259   34523@udel.edu   (302) 555-9292

OBJECTIVE:
Entry level position in the justice system.

EDUCATION:
Bachelor of Arts in Criminal Justice
    University of Delaware, Newark Delaware   (May, 2000)
    G.P.A. 3.1/4.0, National Sociology Honor Society
    Dean's List   (1999-2000)

    Relevant Courses: Criminal Law; Criminal Procedures; Criminal Justice
    Policy; Written and Oral Communications; Business Information Systems

    Study in Madrid, Spain   (Winter, 1998)
    Coursework in Spanish Judicial Systems

SKILLS:
Microsoft Office (Word, Excel, and Power Point)
Delaware Justice Information System
Basic knowledge of Spanish

RELATED EXPERIENCE:
Volunteer, State Department of Justice, Victim/Witness Services Unit, Dover, DE
    Worked with victims of personal and property crimes. Explained criminal
    procedures and court processes. Received specialized training in domestic
    violence. Conducted survey of misdemeanor cases.   (Spring, 2000)

Intern, Court of Common Pleas, Wilmington, DE
    Observed and assisted Clerk of the Court in analyzing efficiency of
    court scheduling. Trained in court procedures.   (Spring, 1999)

Teaching Assistant, Crime and Society (CJ303)   (Fall, 1998)

BUSINESS EXPERIENCE:
Server, The Ground Round, Newark, DE   (Summer, 1998,99)
Customer Service, Newark Video, Newark, DE
    Trained in theft prevention techniques.   (Summer, 1997)

ACTIVITIES:
Intramural Basketball   (1997-present)
    • Captain   (1999)
Special Olympics   (1998-1999)
Campus Security Patrol   (Fall, 1999)
Tutor, Academic Services   (1997)

References Available Upon Request

CHAPTER 12

■■■■■■■■■■■■■■■■■■■■■■

QUESTIONS ABOUT QUESTIONS

"Interviewing is a skill that can be practiced,
perfected, and used to tremendous advantage,
time and time again."

—Diane Berk

Interview Basics

Q: I want to do some role-playing with friends to prepare for some upcoming interviews. What kind of questions should I expect?

A: Congrats—preparing for interviews is an often overlooked, but very important step of the job-search process. Don't practice answers to the point they sound rehearsed, but do consider the key points you want to make in response to typical questions. Of course, interview questions vary greatly depending on your field and level of experience, and whether you are applying for a part-time job while in school, or for a full-time job after graduation. Some basics, however, include the following:

- What are your strengths and weaknesses?
- Why did you choose your major?
- What motivates you?
- How do you respond to pressure?
- What do you do in your free time?
- What accomplishment has given you the most satisfaction?

If you are interviewing for an internship you may also hear some of the following:

- What types of academic and other school-related commitments do you have that might interfere with this position?

• What school activities have you participated in that might
prepare you for your role here at XYZ Inc?

• How will this internship help you achieve your professional goals?

• Which of your current courses is your favorite?

Q: I've had three interviews for co-op placements, and all three started
with "tell me about yourself." How can I answer such a vague
question? What kind of information should I give?

A: We know it's uncreative and open-ended, but the dreaded "tell me
about yourself" question is here to stay. Do a little prep work and
come up with some brief points that describe who you are. You may
mention your major, minor, special interests and skills, year in school,
a few of your in-school activities, and where you are from originally.
Use good judgement, however, and avoid potentially sensitive topics
like religion, political affiliation, or sexual orientation.

Co-op and Internship Interviews

Q: My friend is setting up an "informational interview" at a place she
wants to intern. What is this—and should I be setting them up?

A: In the internship arena, an "informational interview" is a get-to-know-
you meeting set up at an institution where you would like to intern,
when no position is currently available. If you wanted to intern at the
National Association of Experiential Learning Authors, for instance,
you would call to ask if they operate an internship program. If they
do, but you have missed the application deadline, find out the name of
the internship coordinator. Then, send a letter expressing your interest
in being considered for the next round of internships, briefly stating
your qualifications, and requesting a short meeting to learn more
about the program and the association. Call in a week or so to follow
up, and set up an appointment.

If the National Association of Experiential Learning Authors does
not host an internship program (which would be ironic…) find out
who heads the department that interests you. Then, send a similar
letter, but this time include information on the type of internship you
envision, and the skills you would like to learn. Again, be sure to
follow up via phone in a week or so.

Q: My interviewer asked me how many hours per week I can commit to my internship—but I have no idea what's reasonable. Help!

A: Keeping in mind that school is still your first priority, a reasonable internship schedule should include 10-15 hours over a five day week. If you are willing to cut down on your co-curricular activities, you may be able to squeeze in 15-20 hours/week, but under no circumstances should you carry both a full academic load, and more than 20 hours/week at a part time job or internship—something will suffer.

Your answer should be within one of these ranges, based on your other commitments. Tell your potential employer "I am willing to commit between X and Z number of hours per week, will need a more flexible schedule during exam periods, and will be gone during semester breaks. While school is my first priority, I am dependable and will let you know about potential time conflicts with as much advance notice as possible."

Q: I had a great interview for an co-op position I really want, and they offered me the job at the conclusion of the interview. I felt a lot of pressure to make a decision on the spot—is that a good idea? How should I have responded?

A: Don't let pressure force you to make a decision you aren't ready for. The job may look great, but set aside time to discuss your decision with friends and family, and to weigh the pros and cons for yourself. Never accept a job—even the ambassadorship to Bermuda—on the spot. Be sure the internship, work environment, and salary are just as wonderful after a good night's sleep.

How do you get that time without offending your potential boss? A simple "This is a wonderful opportunity, and this seems like a great place to work. Can I let you know in two or three days?" should suffice. If two or three days is too long, ask for at least one day to think it over. Overnight is still too long? Be suspicious of any employer who refuses to allow you time for proper consideration—is this someone for whom you really want to work?

Transitioning to Interviews for Full-Time Work

Q: I've held two internships while in college, plus I worked part-time on campus. Now I am interviewing for full-time jobs. How will these interviews differ?

A: First off, expect longer, more formal interviews with a detailed discussion of your qualifications, work style and background. Most full-time jobs come with salary ranges—not a set stipend or hourly wage. That means you should be prepared to tackle the salary issue and have a general idea of the compensation you require. While your past interviews may have been one-on-one with the internship coordinator, full-time interviews are likely to include sessions with potential supervisors and co-workers—either as a group or one or two at a time.

Q: I sent out resumes for a number of jobs, one of which I am ecstatic about. I was just offered a job by one of the employers, but my "dream job" interview isn't until next week. Should I chuck my "sure thing"—which is a passable position—and hold out for the ideal, or should I give up on my dream job and take the offer on the table?

A: Don't give up your dream just yet! It is perfectly acceptable to ask Job 1 for a week to consider their offer. The day after you interview with Job 2, call to get a sense of their timeline and interest in you. Speak to the person (or one of the people) you interviewed with, thank her for her time, then let her know you have been offered another position. Reaffirm your sincere interest in the position with her company, and tell her you would like to give Job 1 a sense of when you'll have a decision.

Judging from her response, you'll know if you should hold out ("We'll have an offer out by noon tomorrow") or if their interest in you does not warrant waiting ("Well, we won't be through with our search for three weeks. Then we'll start calling for second interviews. I'll let you know then if you will be one of them.").

Interview Attire

Q: Okay, I've got a great resume, wrote some killer cover letters, and have done mock interviews at the career center. One last question—what the heck should I wear?

A: "Don't judge a book by its cover" aside (though we're pretty proud of ours...), appearances are important in the job-hunt process, so shed that student image. Leave the backpack, Birks, and cargo pants on campus, and don a comfortable outfit, within some general guidelines. Internship, co-op or part-time job interviews call for a professional look—but are more relaxed than full-time job interviews. For men, a sport coat, slacks and a tie is an appropriate combination. Women may wear a skirt and blouse, with or without a blazer.

Exceptions include interviews for internships in the financial or legal fields. In those, and other more conservative professions, you should dress as you would for a full-time interview; women should wear a well-fitted wool or wool-blend suit in black, beige, navy, burgundy or gray. The same goes for men, though they should limit their suit colors to dark blues and grays. The jury is still out on pant suits for women—so use good judgement based on the career field and the employer. Conservative professions, or buttoned-down offices, tend to prefer traditional skirt-blazer-shell combinations. When in doubt err on the conservative side. Finish the outfit with simple, dark shoes (pumps or low-heels for women—no flats) and a leather-type briefcase or portfolio. Keep make-up, perfume (and cologne) to a minimum.

Q: I will be interviewing during the summer. Should I sweat it out in a wool suit, or are there appropriate alternatives?

A: If you are interviewing for an internship or simply a summer job, you have some leeway—a cool skirt and blouse, or a lightweight sportcoat and unlined slacks should keep you from pouring sweat. The news is not so good if you are applying for full-time postgraduate work. If you can stand a wool blend—cooler than 100% sheep—do so. Otherwise, a professional looking rayon suit can suffice. Steer clear of linen or cotton, unless the look is crisp and corporate (remember, they wrinkle easily). Despite the heat, women hunting full-time jobs should wear pantyhose and avoid sleeveless blazers.

Money Talk

Q: I get uncomfortable when interviewers ask me for my "salary history." This will be my first full-time job, so I don't really have a salary history. Do I have to answer this question?

A: You are under no obligation to answer any of your interviewer's questions, but if you want the job, you should. Tell your interviewer your ending salary at your last two jobs, and mention that they were part-time jobs, internships, or summer employment. A reasonable professional understands he/she can't pay you the same amount as an administrative assistant as you earned at the campus ice cream shack.

Q: This is my first time looking for a "real job," and I have no idea what kind of salary to expect. What do I say if my interviewer asks for my salary requirements?

A: Your "salary requirement" doesn't just mean the minimum you can live on. It means the amount of money that is reasonable for the position, the field, your geographic area, and your level of experience. An afternoon of research in your college's career library will provide you with the information you need. When the question is asked, politely reply, "What has the salary for this position typically been?" Then, given your research and their answer, you should be able to provide a salary requirement range, spanning two to three thousand dollars.

Q: If the interview is wrapping up, and we still haven't discussed salary, can I bring it up? How?

A: If your potential employer hasn't raised the salary issue, leave it for a follow-up interview or discuss it once you have been offered the job.

Site Seeing

Name of Site

http://www.jnhg.com/interviewing.htm

Offers information on all types of interviews as well as the typical stages of the interviewing process.

University of Buffalo Career Office

http://www.ub-careers.buffalo.edu/nfcpa/trd/tips.htm

Helpful hints about the art and science of interviewing.

CareerPlanIt

http://www.careerplanit.com/dept/choices/re_inform.htm

A great source for learning more about the process of information interviewing.

Career Magazine

http://www.careermag.com/newsarts/interviewing.html

Here's a collection of articles about interviewing and other topics by experts in the field.

Print Resources

Job Interviewing for College Students, John D. Shingleton, VGM Career Horizons, 1996.

Knock 'em Dead 1998, Martin Yate, Peregrine McCoy Ltd., 1998

The 250 Job Interview Questions You'll Most Likely Be Asked, Peter Veruki, Adams Media Corporation, 1999.

CHAPTER 13

■■■■■■■■■■■■■■■■■■■■

FINAL THOUGHTS:
THE JOB MARKET AND YOU

"Be yourself, nobody else qualifies."

—John Crystal

"Nothing is certain except change." Stated more than two thousand years ago by Greek philosopher, Heraclitus, these ancient words still ring true, especially for today's college students. We live in an uncertain and changing world. You have probably been told that not only can you expect to change jobs six to nine times in the course of your working life, but you are also likely to completely revamp your occupation three or more times! Your first job out of college is certainly a defining moment in your life, but it is not a lifetime commitment—merely a starting point.

Case Study ════════════════════════════

Maria almost didn't major in communications (in pursuit of her dream of becoming a TV news reporter) because she kept hearing about the low salaries and tight job market faced by young graduates in many communications-related fields. Before she made a final decision, however, she got in touch with a young professional who was employed in the television industry to gather some "real-life" information. Paul Johnson, a news reporter for an ABC affiliate, talked to Maria at length about the importance of the work he did at his college TV station, developing and polishing the skills he needed to launch his career. An internship at the Public Broadcasting System provided him with additional experience and contacts.

"Even with all my experience and good recommendations, it was hard landing that first job right out of college," admitted Paul, and the pay was pretty low, but I just needed to get a foot in the door. I knew that I could prove myself, if I was just given the chance. TV news was definitely the field for me and nothing was going to stop me." Four years and two jobs later, Paul has landed a job he loves with an impressive salary.

After her conversation with Paul Johnson, Maria understood that if she wanted to make her career dreams come true, she would have to enhance her employability by taking part in related activities during college which would build her skill-set and qualify her for a position in T.V. news. She also learned that entry level salaries could be boosted by experience and competence over a relatively short period of time. With this in mind, Maria decided to stay with a field about which she felt passionate.

This is not your parents' or grandparents' job market. The landscape of the world of work has undergone rapid change. Corporate mergers, reorganization, technological advances, and a swiftly changing global market are re-writing the outdated paradigm of steady advancement up the corporate ladder working for one organization. The current job market is ablaze with new job titles, new styles of working, and new possibilities. Unemployment is low and salaries are climbing. At the same time, new flexibility has brought instability to the job market. Not only is there no assurance that your job will still exist in a year, there are no guarantees that this growth in the job market as a whole will last over the long term.

The World of Work

With the old rules changing and the future uncertain, there is the natural tendency to try to seize control, to pick the ideal major, to choose the perfect recession-proof career: lucrative, geographically-portable, and eternally in high demand. With this unrealistic, but understandable objective in mind, many students and their parents anxiously seek out information about the "hot careers,"—career fields where the need is great and the supply of qualified workers is inadequate to meet the growing demand, resulting in high job availability and fat salaries. Statistical information about where recent alumni work and how much they earn is readily available from college admission or career services offices. You can also check the Bureau of Labor Statistics' *Occupational Outlook Handbook*, in print or on-line, to locate national projections for job growth and salary trends across a wide variety of occupations.

While you shouldn't ignore or minimize the implications of job market trends, neither should you pick your major and approach your college experience only as a means of job training. Your college experience should be multidimensional—a golden opportunity to expand your knowledge base, clarify your values, try out new ideas, and express your creativity. Your unique "package" of aptitudes, values, interests, and skills should determine which curriculum you choose to follow and what activities you elect to pursue. That said, early and repeated visits to the college career center to explore career options, and a workable plan to take full advantage of your college's second curriculum will go a long way toward ensuring your marketability at graduation in any and all fields.

Top Ten

Each Fall, the National Association of Colleges and Employers (NACE) surveys employers to determine what skills and abilities new graduates of all majors need to be prepared for entry level employment. The most recent survey results identify these top ten characteristics as critically important for new hires: Communications skills, Work experience, Motivation/ Initiative, Teamwork skills, Leadership abilities, High grade point average/

academic credentials, Technical/computer skills, Interpersonal skills, Analytical skills, and Ethics.

Savvy students who want to capture the attention of employers will take full advantage of both the standard academic curriculum and second curriculum to acquire and polish these skills during their undergraduate years, and learn to showcase them when it comes time to job-hunt.

Go for Your Dream

You must take the responsibility for developing your own individual job market, irrespective of major or job goals. The well-known career consultant, Richard Bolles, points out that every day, there are job vacancies in most fields and geographic areas. All over America, companies are creating new positions, and employees are earning promotions, retiring, or moving on to fill job vacancies elsewhere. If you have a passion to pursue a job in a low-demand, low-growth field, don't let your plans be derailed by gloomy economic forecasts. Just make sure you acquire the skills, experience and recommendations to be the most competitive candidate possible. Remember, the difference between the so-called "hot" and "cold" occupations is the *degree of competition* you will experience in searching out a position that meets your needs and goals. While you should certainly review statistical information about job availability, keep in mind that there are no perfect majors, no perfect strategies, and no perfect careers, except those at which you personally will excel.

Students and parents sometimes forget that college is about much more than preparation for your first "real world" job after graduation. College is about widening your horizons, expanding your possibilities, and educating yourself for *every* job and *every* activity you will ever pursue.

The ball is now in your court—so use your college experience as a "learning laboratory" to develop and practice skills that will be useful in your personal, professional, and community experiences over your lifetime. You now know the formula for success.

Good luck!

ABOUT THE AUTHORS

Anthony J. Arcieri

Anthony Arcieri is Residential Academic Coordinator at George Mason University in Fairfax, Virginia where he develops academic initiatives and "living and learning" programs in the residence halls. Prior to that, Mr. Arcieri worked in both career and academic services at the University of Delaware. He has also worked in academic advising, residential life, and admissions at The George Washington University in Washington DC.

Mr. Arcieri holds a masters degree in Student Affairs Practice in Higher Education from the University of Delaware, and a Bachelor of Arts in Political Science from The George Washington University. He is also an experienced presenter on resume writing, job hunting techniques, "the internship experience," and interview preparation.

Marianne Green

Marianne Green has served as Assistant Director of the Career Services Center at the University of Delaware since 1985 where she manages placement and field experience programs and counsels students on their career development. Prior to that she directed the Career Planning and Placement office at Rocky Mountain College in Billings, Montana.

She holds masters degrees in counseling and education from Washington University in St. Louis, Missouri and Xavier University in Cincinnati, Ohio and a Bachelor of Arts in English from Goucher College in Towson, Maryland. Ms. Green is the author of *Internship Success*, published by VGM Horizons and numerous articles and book reviews on career-related subjects for the *Journal of Career Planning and Employment* and other publications.

College Planning Guides from Octameron

Don't Miss Out: The Ambitious Student's Guide to Financial Aid $9.00
Hailed as the top consumer guide to student aid, *Don't Miss Out* covers scholarships, loans, and personal finance strategies. It will save readers hundreds, if not thousands of dollars in college costs.

The A's and B's of Academic Scholarships $9.00
Money for being bright! This book describes 100,000 awards offered by nearly 1200 colleges. Best of all, most of these (which must be used at the sponsoring school) are not based on financial need.

Loans and Grants from Uncle Sam $6.00
Increase your eligibility for federal student aid. This guide describes it all—the aid application process as well as loans and grants for students, parents and health professionals.

SAT Savvy: Last Minute Tips and Strategies $6.00
Nervous about the SAT? Whether you took a test prep course or are relying on innate ability, SAT Savvy contains all the tips you need to boost your confidence and your scores.

Majoring in Success: Building Your Career While Still in College $8.00
While in college, think beyond courses, grades and majors. Take advantage of internships, work-study, campus activities, volunteerism and cooperative education to offset college costs, connect with future employers, build a strong resume, prepare for job interviews, and much more.

Financial Aid Officers: What They Do—To You and For You $5.00
Should you accept your award package as offered? Can you request it be changed, or increased? Knowledgeable dealings with FAOs can result in more money. This book shows you how.

Behind the Scenes: An Inside Look at the College Admission Process $5.00
Ed Wall, former Dean of Admission at Amherst College, offers sage advice and detailed profiles of successful applicants. An invaluable view from inside on how the selection process really works.

Do It Write: How to Prepare a Great College Application $6.00
Personalize your essays so they stand out from the crowd. Author Gary Ripple is the former Admission Director at Lafayette College and the College of William and Mary

College Match: A Blueprint for Choosing the Best School for You $8.00
Author Steve Antonoff combines dozens of easy-to-use worksheets with lots of practical advice to make sure you find schools that meet your needs and your preferences.

Campus Pursuit: Making the Most of the Visit and Interview $5.00
Nervous about your interview? In his companion book to *Do-It Write*, Gary Ripple gives advice that will help you shine, as well as show you how to maximize the benefits of a campus visit.

College.edu: On-Line Resources for the Cyber-Savvy Student $8.00
Lost in Cyberspace? *College.edu* takes you to hundreds of useful sites on admission and financial aid, giving you Internet tips and warnings along the way.

Campus Daze: Easing the Transition from High School to College $5.00
Learn what to expect during your first year of college and how to succeed starting on Day One. Author George Gibbs is the former Dean of Admission and Freshmen at Muhlenberg College.

Financial Aid FinAncer: Expert Answers to College Financing Questions $6.00
Learn how special family circumstances impact on student aid.

The Winning Edge: The Student-Athlete's Guide to College Sports $6.00
It's all here. Scholarship opportunities. NCAA rules and regulations. Advice from coaches. Sample athletic resumes. Strategies, timetables, and worksheets—all to help you take your sport to college!

College Savings R_x: Investment Prescriptions for a Healthy College Fund $8.00
Short- and long-term college planning strategies from investment expert David G. Speck, a Managing Director for Wheat First Union.

Calculating Expected Family Contribution (EFC) Software $42.00
Now it's easy to play "what if" games with your expected family contribution. This Windows 95/98 compatible CD-Rom software is adapted from the worksheets found in *Don't Miss Out*.

Ordering Information

Send orders to: Octameron Associates, PO Box 2748, Alexandria, VA 22301, or contact us at: 703-836-5480 (voice), 703-836-5650 (fax), or http://www.octameron.com (Internet). **Postage and Handling:** Please include $3.00 for the first publication, $1.00 for each additional, to a maximum of $5.00 per order. **Method of Payment:** Payment must accompany order. We accept checks, money orders, Visa and MasterCard. If ordering by credit card, please include the card number and its expiration date.